DATE DUE

			PRINTED IN U.S.A.

Twentieth Century Library

Franz Boas

MELVILLE J. HERSKOVITS

Franz Boas

THE SCIENCE OF MAN
IN THE MAKING

CHARLES SCRIBNER'S SONS, NEW YORK

CHARLES SCRIBNER'S SONS, LTD., LONDON

1953

ACKNOWLEDGMENTS

It is a pleasure to acknowledge the assistance given me in the preparation of this work by the staff of Deering Library, Northwestern University, where the Boas reprint collection is housed; to Mr. Albert C. Gerould, Librarian of Clark University, for making available the rare copies of early catalogues of that institution, covering the years when Boas taught there; to Mr. Henry McCurdy of the Macmillan Company, New York, for sending to me the file of reviews of the second edition of Boas' *Mind of Primitive Man*, and of his *Race, Language and Culture*; and to Dr. Alexander Lesser, Executive Director of the Association on Indian Affairs, with whom I was able to check my impressions concerning Boas' participation in programs of action having to do with the American Indian.

M. J. H.

Evanston, Illinois
7 November, 1952

CONTENTS

Franz Boas

CHAPTER ONE

FROM THE COLOR OF WATER
TO THE STUDY OF MAN

ON the 20th of June, 1883, the schooner *Germania,* a veteran of the polar seas, sailed once more from Hamburg, bound for the far north. In 1869–70 she had transported an expedition to East Greenland, and in 1882 the personnel of a German polar station had travelled in her. Now she was returning, to bring these men home after their long winter's isolation. And this time she carried a young physicist-geographer and his servant, on their way to Cumberland Sound.

The young physicist-geographer was Franz Boas, and his trip was to have consequences far beyond its immediate objective of geographical exploration. For in the hard Arctic winter he was to spend with the Eskimos, Boas was to discover values in their personalities and ways of life that constituted a challenge he would devote the rest of his life to meeting.

Three years after his return, he wrote this paragraph: ". . . After a long and intimate intercourse with the Eskimo, it was with feelings of sorrow and regret that I parted from my Arctic friends. I had seen that they enjoyed life, and a hard life, as we do; that nature is also beautiful to them; that feelings of friendship also root in the Eskimo heart; that, although the character of their life is so rude as compared to civilized life, the Eskimo is a man as we are; that his feelings, his virtues and his shortcomings are based in human nature, like ours."

Here are foreshadowed many of the questions that were to

1

dominate Boas' scientific inquiry down the long years to come, and to inform his teaching. Why should men of differing physical type, living in different climates, differ so strikingly in their modes of existence, and yet be so similar in other ways? Does their innate physical endowment, their race, determine their behavior? How does the nature of the habitat affect the institutions, beliefs, and accepted forms of conduct found in human societies? To what extent can men of one physical type be held inherently superior to those of another, or inferior? To what extent can it be said that one way of life, or culture, is better than another? Can the achievements of a people be regarded as adequate criteria of their level of development? Or should their achievements be thought of as particular manifestations of the human adventure, worked out during the millennia man had existed on earth? Can civilizations be evaluated on the grounds of technical competence and economic complexity? Or are these but restricted areas of human achievement, of no more and no less value than accomplishments in the arts, in the adjustment of human relations, or in drawing consistent and logical explanations of the world and the powers that direct it?

We need only think back three quarters of a century, when the passage we have quoted was written, and consider some of the events that have occurred since, to grasp the significance of the problems Boas was raising when he wrote it. This was the height of the Victorian era, when the supremacy of the European way of life was never more taken for granted. Even for Boas the superiority of European "civilization" was so implicit that he could write of the character of Eskimo life as ". . . rude as compared to civilized life"—a phrase that, in the light of the development of his thought, startles those who know only his later writings.

This penultimate decade of the Nineteenth Century was a critical one in the history of European contacts with the rest of the world. Together with the one that succeeded it, it saw the theory of the primacy of the white race and of European civilization reach its greatest acceptance. It witnessed the rapid extension of European political control over the world, when the feeling that colonial possessions were a liability had given way to the conviction that they were an asset to the national economy, a road to national power, and a necessity for national prestige. During this short time Africa was partitioned, European control in Asia consolidated, the islands of the Pacific became part of the overseas possessions of the colonial powers.

It was during this time, too, that earlier discussions concerning the differences between human groupings having different physical characteristics began to take on new and far-reaching significance. The rationalizations for Negro slavery that had agitated the intellectual world of America and Europe a quarter-century earlier were by no means laid to rest because of the military victory which dictated the end of the system in the United States, and doomed it in the other parts of the New World where it still persisted. Earlier, in France, Count de Gobineau had laid the groundwork for a theory of racial superiority that was to be applied, not to extra-European peoples, but to the sub-racial types of Europe itself. If, in the New World, racism was to rationalize Negro slavery; in the Old it was to furnish the conceptual base for an increasingly active anti-Semitism that for centuries had ebbed and flowed, and which Boas himself must have experienced in his University career and later.

Both the theories of cultural and racial inferiority, implicitly questioned by Boas in his earliest anthropological writings and later challenged by him with the rich documentation he was to bring to bear in support of his position, have, certainly in no small measure because of his work, come under severe attack. The acceptance of the "higher" character of Euroamerican civilization that marked the early domination of peoples deemed inferior by those who ruled them, has been replaced by doubt. India, Indonesia, Lybia, the Gold Coast, clearly point to, as they have in part resulted from, the rejection of the theory of cultural superiority, in many instances by rulers no less than by those ruled.

The ethnocentrism of Victorian and post-Victorian days, however, is by no means a thing of the past, any more than is the racism which reached its culmination in the concepts that dominated Nazi Germany. Certainly the destruction of Nazism did much to discredit the theory that, if so complex a development can be ascribed so simply, gave drive and direction to the quest for world dominance which eventually made it necessary to oppose force with force, and resulted in the holocaust of the Second World War. Yet here, too, as in the case of the theory of cultural superiority, the tide of bigotry, seemingly always gathering strength, was being consistently opposed by making known the scientific fallacies on which it rested. And in this, too, the position of Boas, foreshadowed in his early reports on the Eskimo and his subsequent research, his writing and his University lecturing, were intellectual factors of major significance. It should not be forgotten that in the burning of the books which marked Nazi accession to power, one of the volumes that was physically, though never spiritually, consumed, was his *Kultur und Rasse.*

2

The paths Boas was to follow in working out the implications of his early recognition of the fact that similarities, no less than differences, exist between men, and his quest for an understanding of their nature and significance, were independently trod. They led him into every field of anthropological research, and brought him to understand and stress the essential unity in the study of man, whether it concerned physical type or learned behavior, the role of language in culture or the prehistoric past. In many cases, before any positive contribution could issue, he had to clear away earlier hypotheses that proved untenable in the light of the evidence he could marshal. In others, his own pioneering gave rise to dispute by those who questioned his departure from long-sanctioned procedures. In many areas, however, his ideas and the data he assembled were accepted without reserve.

His most famous book, *The Mind of Primitive Man,* was an attempt to answer the knotty problem of the relation between human physical type and culture. It was foreshadowed in two addresses. The first of these, delivered in 1894, when Boas was vice-president of the American Association for the Advancement of Science, was entitled "Human Faculty as Determined by Race." Its initial paragraphs were carried over almost unchanged, to introduce the book published fifteen years later. The second, delivered in 1900, when Boas was president of the American Folklore Society, represents his first use of the well-known title.

This volume, published in 1911, soon became a classic of American social science. It was well known in England; it was the German version that was burned by the Nazis. Though in no sense a textbook, it was read and studied by generations of college students, to say nothing of the general readers who turned to it to clarify their thinking on this confused problem, or the many others who read excerpts from it in the numberless works in which it was quoted. The effect of any single volume on an historic stream of the proportions of American race prejudice is, of course, difficult to trace. It is enough to say, with Frederick Wood-Jones, who in 1938 reviewed the second edition, that while "in 1895 the audience were impressed far more by its daring than by an orthodoxy that now seems so apparent . . . there were few prepared to see in his writings, regarded at the time as somewhat speculative, that background of common sense that seems so conspicuous to the reader of today."

Boas' discussions of the relation between race and culture, considered in the large, continued to exert their steady pressure toward interracial and cross-cultural understanding and tolerance, but some of his specific researches in this field brought on sharp controversy. Outstanding in this regard was his study of the changes in the bodily form of the descendants of immigrants, made for the Dillingham Commission of the United States Senate and published in 1910. The question of the "melting pot," taking its name from the novel by Israel Zangwill, was being much debated. Immigration was bringing millions of prospective new citizens to the United States. Could these numbers be assimilated to the existing body of American citizens? Above all, could this conglomerate afford the basis for a coherent and unified population? As scientific research, Boas' method of comparing measurements of parents and children by the use of biometric techniques was a daring innovation. Its results challenged the dogma of the day, that the physical type of any organism is determined by hereditary, genetic components alone and that environmental forces were unable to affect the end result of their functioning.

The political debate over immigration was centered on practical issues of an economic and social nature far more than on the biological aspects. While it went on, the immigrants continued to come in vast numbers, until the matter was temporarily settled for the United States when the outbreak of the First World War effectively dried up the stream. When these clouds had disappeared, the question was reshaped. The melting pot was no longer the point debated, but racial superiority and inferiority. From any practical point of view, Boas' "head-form study," as it came to be called, was not germane, since on this level the battle was fought along broader lines. But the head-form study was not forgotten in the scientific world and, as we shall see, the arguments it generated continued for many years.

Boas' interest in understanding man in all the varied manifestations of his existence gave rise to research in areas where controversy, if any, was more restrained, and concerned technical points of method or concept. His independence of thought in these areas of his interest led to some of his outstanding evaluations and contributions, which can only be named at this point in our discussion. The study of the dynamics of culture, which came to be one of the most important concerns of cultural anthropology, owes much to his insistence on the careful, intensive study of changes in the habits of life of peoples living in restricted areas, subject to historical and natural influences that can be scientifically assessed. The stress he laid on the importance of psychological factors in culture has become common among anthropologists who, with but a few exceptions, think of culture as at base a psychological phenomenon. The principle that each element in a culture must be analyzed in terms of its relationship to other aspects of the totality of which it is a part was implicit in all his work. This is one reason why functionalism, an anthropological doctrine much debated during the decade from 1925 to 1935, seemed to Boas and those trained by him but a sharpening of well-established conventions of field research.

He early saw the significance of taking into full account the historical component in culture, and was at the forefront of those who combatted the transfer of principles of biological evolution to the manifestations of man's learned behavior. The controversy whether anthropology is a science or an historical discipline, endemic among anthropologists, touched him not at all. As early as 1904 he realized that this debate was not subject to resolution by the methods of scholarship. His realistic approach to this, as to other problems, is well indicated by the way in which, in a discussion entitled "The History of Anthropology," he summarized the point at issue; "As in other sciences where subject matter is the actual distribution of phenomena and their causal relation, we find in anthropology two distinct methods of research and aims of investigation; the one, the historical method, which endeavors to reconstruct the actual history of mankind; the other, the generalizing method, which attempts to establish the laws of its development. According to the personal inclination of the investigator, the one or the other method prevails in his researches."

The comprehensiveness of Boas' approach to the study of man, and his sense of problem, are nowhere better exemplified than in his continued concern with the humanistic aspects of anthropological science, a position strikingly at variance with the sociological emphasis laid by so many of his later contemporaries. He early recognized the importance of language as a factor in the study of culture, and the need to discover the range of variation in its structure and functioning. The innovations he introduced in this field were revolutionary, and have given rise to an entire discipline, that of comparative linguistics. This realization was certainly not unrelated to his experience among the Eskimo, nor was the interest he displayed in the study of the graphic and plastic arts, the music and dance, either of those peoples among whom he carried on field research, or in terms of a broader comparative scale. The oral arts, as well, claimed his interest. He was a founding member of the American Folk-lore Society, and for years he edited its *Journal*.

Yet in all his work, whatever its approach, he continuously stressed the innate worth of the human being, the dignity of all human culture. Typical of this is the introductory statement in his volume *Primitive Art*: "The treatment . . . is based on two principles that, I believe, should guide all investigations into the manifestations of life among primitive people: the one being the fundamental sameness of mental processes in all races and in all cultural forms of the present day; the other, the consideration of every cultural phenomenon as the result of historical happenings." Again and again, in this work as always in his writings, he rejects any hypothesis that ascribes differences in cultural phenomena to different kinds or degrees of mental ability.

This point of view, though it is suggested in Boas' earliest writings, was a matter of growth and development. He struggled for many years to sharpen his concept of the term "primitive," a word that is being increasingly rejected in favor of less connotative designations for the peoples without written languages who have classically been the subject for anthropological study. Certainly, when we consider the prevailing climate of opinion, it is not strange that in 1894 Boas would contrast the "wonderful achievements" of "civilized man" with those of the "humbler members of mankind," with their "meagre achievements" who had not "succeeded in subduing nature, who labor to eke a meagre existence out of the products of the wilderness; who hear with trembling the roar of the wild animals and see the products of their toil destroyed by them; who remain restricted by ocean, river or mountains; who strive to obtain the necessities of life with the help of few and simple instruments." What is remarkable is the caution he sounds as to the interpretation of these differences. "As the civilization is higher, we assume that the aptitude for civilization is also higher. . . . In this conclusion . . . the achievement and the aptitude for an achievement has been confounded." And in 1938, when the *Mind of Primitive Man* was revised, these passages were omitted, in favor of a simple statement of the fact of differences between men in physical type and culture, and the need to clarify the significance of the differences and the relationships between the two aspects of the human organism.

The credo Boas had developed, both as regards science and its place in society, is found in four sentences in the preface to this revision, which in terms of "the results of his studies" he feels have yielded "an ever-increasing certainty of his conclusions." These are the sentences: "There is no fundamental difference in the ways of thinking of primitive and civilized man. A close connection between race and personality has never been established. The concept of racial type as commonly used even in scientific literature is misleading and requires a logical, as well as a biological definition. . . . The suppression of intellectual freedom rings the death knell of science."

3

Why Boas embarked on his trip to the Arctic has never been satisfactorily explained. His work for the doctorate had been in physics, with a minor in geography. His doctoral thesis, published in 1881, was entitled *Contribution to the Understanding of the Color of Water (Beiträge zur Erkenntniss der Farbe des Wassers).* Only in one way does the thin pamphlet of forty-two pages foreshadow any aspect of Boas' later mass of publication—in the leanness and austerity of its prose, and its disdain of any of those devices that ease the effort of the reader. At the outset, as through the whole of his career, Boas held that the data and their implications were alone worthy of attention. If important conclusions were to fall in the middle of a paragraph deep in a chapter of a book, or at the center of an article, it was the business of the reader to find them for himself. This is apparent in his thesis, which devotes its concluding paragraph to an acknowledgement of those who aided him in the ordering of his research.

Legend among his students and associates had it that the logic of his problem forced him to seek its ultimate answer in the psycho-cultural field. It was recounted how he came to recognize that one factor in determining perceptions of the color of water was the body of ideas regarding color held by a people, which is to say, a convention of their culture. He was thus held to have elected to study the remote Eskimo, to find from them the color they saw in the water of the seas about them, and thus, so to speak, take another cultural sight on the question. Boas, himself, did not discourage this interpretation, and in later years would sometimes phrase the problem in this way. One of Boas' students, Ruth Benedict, has even asserted that he went to the Arctic "specifically to study the reaction of the human mind to the natural environment," though this attributes to his research a far broader scope than have others.

There is ample internal evidence, however, that this version is apocryphal. Boas' expedition to the Arctic, as planned, was essentially geographical. He wished to perfect the mapping of the region, and the eventual ethnographic character of his research seems to have developed during the time he was there, as an intensification of an interest which has been ascribed by some to the influence of one of his teachers, Theobald Fischer, in encouraging an interest in cultural geography. Moreover, the question of the perception of the color of water by the Eskimo does not enter into any of the reports of his work published during the years 1884 to 1888, when the definitive monograph he wrote covering his studies appeared as one of the early volumes of the Bureau of American Ethnology. The question, indeed, was never raised at all by him, either as concerns the Eskimo or any of the other peoples he later studied. In a paper published in 1936, where he discusses his early interests, he says no more than that while "it is quite true that as a young man I devoted my time to the study of physics and geography . . . I aligned myself clearly with those who are motivated by the affective appeal of a phenomenon that impresses us as a unit, although its elements may be irreducible to a common cause. In other words the problem that attracted me primarily was the intelligent understanding of a complex phenomenon. When from geography my interest was directed to ethnology, the same interest prevailed."

Certainly, if the psycho-cultural factor in the perception of the color of water had seemed important to Boas when he was preparing his dissertation, there would have been ample opportunity to mention it in presenting the six theses which, in addition to the problem of his research, he chose to defend before his examiners. Three of these theses had to do with physical or psychophysical questions under debate at the time. Two, the second and fifth, which foreshadowed his immediate and his later interest, were geographical, one asserting that Greenland does not extend north of the 83rd parallel, the other that geography is basic in the study of history. The sixth thesis, which ranged farthest afield, maintained that "modern operetta is reprehensible from the standpoint of art and morality."

But if his doctoral dissertation and his initial ethnographic researches among the Eskimo do not give us the answer to the problem of why his interests shifted from physics to anthropology, they do reveal many of the traits of Boas' personality that were to make of him the figure he became. We see here his scientific integrity and intransigence, that made compromise on any level unthinkable. We see his fertility of mind and his ability to grasp and phrase a problem, that caused him to develop the many innovations in theoretical analysis and methodological techniques for which he became famous. We see the mathematical ability that gave the analytic bent to his approach to all questions, and the point of view which insisted that theory not outrun inductively derived proof. But also, in that one of his theses wherein he holds for the undesirable character of *"moderne Operette,"* we see Boas the humanist, the romanticist, the traditionalist. As with all men, he was the creature of his times; but as a creative, critical scholar he compounded in his personality the complexities which even in the ordinary individual are sufficiently intricate.

4

Boas was born in the town of Minden, in northwestern Germany, on July 9, 1858, and lived there until he entered on his University career nineteen years later. His associations with his birthplace were pleasant; his book-plate frames a picture of a principal structure of the town. His family were in good circumstances. His father was a merchant; his mother, we are told, founded the first Froebel Kindergarten there. A younger sister of his mother married a physician, Dr. Abraham Jacobi, who came from a nearby community, and who was to have a deep and continuing influence on the course of Boas' personal life, giving him hospitality when he first arrived in the United States, and introducing him to the young woman who later became his wife.

He studied at the Universities of Heidelberg, Bonn and Kiel, participating, we may assume, in the customary activities of the German university student of the time. In the light of his feeling concerning some of the excesses of American college life, it is not without interest to note that he joined one of the student corps that was the equivalent of the fraternities of our day in the United States. He was loyal to it during his later years, as witness the file of its journal *Alemannia* found in his library after his death. He was also a loyal alumnus. Many Universities and academies conferred honorary degrees and honorary memberships on him, but one degree he especially treasured was the honorary Doctorate of Medicine which Kiel awarded him when "renewing" his original diploma. This was in accord with German custom, under which a doctorate is valid only for fifty years, a convention that permits recognition to be given the achievements of a scholar who has devoted his working life to the furtherance of knowledge or to teaching.

Boas first came to the United States in 1884, when he spent the winter in New York on his return from the Arctic. He found the intellectual atmosphere attractive, and the freedom to choose his own way that was denied him in Germany much to his liking. Though he went back to his native land to accept a position in the Ethnological Museum in Berlin, and passed the examination which put him on the initial rung of the academic hierarchy as Docent in Geography, the restrictions of the organization of German intellectual life galled him, and he eventually gave them over for a career in the United States, despite the precarious material foundations on which he was to build it.

His return to North America was without particular thought of such a move, for he came to embark on his second field trip, this time in the Pacific Northwest, among the Bella Coola Indians. The field work was carried on during 1886. In 1887, when in New York on his way home, he was offered, and accepted, a position on *Science*, writing the numerous articles, notes, and reviews —forty-three items in 1887 and the first half of 1888—that crowd his bibliography during the year and a half he held the position. It was scientific hack work, ranging from a review headed "Supan's Journal of Commercial Geography" to an article entitled "The Earth's Rotation as Affecting Railway-Trains," but it gave him time to do his own writing. In 1888 alone he published nineteen contributions in scientific journals, in addition to his monograph *The Central Eskimo,* abstracts of two papers read before the New York Academy of Sciences, and some popular articles, such as the one entitled "Is Stanley Dead?" in *The North American Review.*

The period when he was on the staff of *Science* was an important one for Boas. Because his position yielded him an assured, though slight income, he was enabled to marry. And it was while working for the journal that he obtained his first post in an American institution of higher learning. In a sense, the period marks the beginnings of the two currents of Boas' life, the personal and professional, which stand in such marked contrast—the first calm, conventional, warm in human relations, the second turbulent, courageous, wherein Boas was the supreme individualist, who dominated the scene in which he for so many years played his role.

He left New York during the summer of 1888, going back to the Northwest Coast to continue his research, now for a Committee of the British Association for the Advancement of Science on the Northwestern Tribes of Canada, under the chairmanship of the noted English anthropologist E. B. Tylor. On his return, he went to Cleveland, Ohio, to attend the meeting of the American Association, and, according to the story as he told it, chatted with a gentleman who shared his seat. As the train was coming into the station at Cleveland, his seat-mate introduced himself, and invited him to accept a teaching post in an institution of higher learning then being founded, which he headed. The seat-mate was G. Stanley Hall, and the institution was Clark University at Worcester, Massachusetts. Boas accepted the offer, and remained there for four years.

Here appears a theme in Boas' experience that was to be repeated at various times in the years to follow, contained in incidents that arose in his dealings with those in administrative positions in the institutions where he served. The need to adjust to the requirements of maintaining equable relations with fellow-members of a large organization was never permitted to take precedence over what for him was the paramount demand for truth and fair dealing. Boas likewise insisted on the importance of complete frankness in judging intellectual capacity and integrity, and evaluated all situations in terms of the obligation to discharge his responsibilities, as he saw them, to the fullest. Obviously, to the administrator, charged with achieving a frictionless, efficient operation of an organization, Boas was "difficult" or "non-cooperative"—those most damning of terms where preferment, to say nothing of opportunity, is at stake. Boas, however, conceived of the task of the administrator in any intellectual community to be the servant, not the master, of those who were instrumental in achieving the aims which gave the group its reason for being. In his dealings with such persons, as with those of his colleagues from whom he differed in scientific debate, he permitted no considerations of academic diplomacy to interfere with what he held to be a valid scholarly end or the dictates of honesty.

In actuality there was little nuance in Boas' professional life. If the controversies in which he engaged were acrid, the loyalties he engendered were firm. The attitude of his students toward him, like that of many of his associates, was marked by deep devotion, even though this could be tempered by the ambivalences that arise in the course of the relations between a strong teacher and the student of fertile mind. In times of stress, however, the ambivalences were invariably submerged in the loyalties Boas called forth. Moreover, while he paid in many ways for his intransigence toward administrators, he never lacked for funds for his research. His power of analysis, his fertile inventiveness in the field of method, and his drive assured foundations and research committees that projects of his they supported would be prosecuted with vigor and imagination, and yield significant findings.

The years 1889 to 1892, when Boas was at Clark University, saw his productivity continue undiminished. It was here that he began his work on the problems of human growth and development, initiating what was to be one of his continuing major interests. He plotted the height-weight curves for Worcester children in a study, carried on with Alexander F. Chamberlain, that gained for Chamberlain the first doctorate to be granted in anthropology by an American university, and for Boas initiated a series of studies which provided statistical averages that for years served as a guide to the practical problems of child welfare and child development. While he was at Clark he also conducted annual researches among the Indians of the Northwest Coast, the results appearing in the relevant Reports of the British Association. Other contributions, such as those on linguistics and ethnological theory and method, ranged the fields of anthropology, as they were to do in later years.

At Clark, anthropology was a part of the department of psychology, headed by the President. Boas gave varied courses, laying the foundation for his later repertoire. In 1889–90 he offered "Anthropology of North America," "Methods of Anthropological Investigations," and, as the catalog put it, gave a "seminary on 'Shamanism.' " The following year he gave one course in physical anthropology, one entitled "Anthropology of Africa," and a series of lectures during the spring on "American Myths." In his third year he repeated the course on physical anthropology, and developed a new second offering, "Application of Statistics to Anthropology." Aside from his course-work and his research, he found stimulating associations among his colleagues. G. Stanley Hall had great ability in sensing promise in young men. With Boas on the early faculty were Henry H. Donaldson, the biologist who later became head of the Wistar Institute in Philadelphia, and A. A. Michelson, the physicist who joined the University of Chicago and later achieved world fame for his discoveries of the speed of light. These associations developed into lasting friendships—Boas' younger son was named after Donaldson, while Michelson's son, Truman, known for his work in American Indian linguistics, became one of Boas' followers.

Tensions began to arise at Clark, however. As Boas in later years recounted the precipitating incident, Hall, in one important matter, gave the faculty certain assurances that were at variance with understandings he had reached with the trustees. Boas promptly resigned, and with him went Donaldson, Michelson and others. The intensity of Boas' reaction to what he conceived to be Hall's irresponsibility never diminished, a feeling not lessened by his view as to the inadequacies of Hall's psychological position.

5

The following decade, with its steady increase in family responsibilities, was a difficult one for Boas, though it saw no diminution in his research activities, and a steady stream of publications continued to appear over his name. From Clark he went to Chicago, to be assistant chief of the department of anthropology at the World Columbian Exposition, and later Curator of anthropology in the permanent institution that eventually was to become the Chicago Natural History Museum. He left the latter when, as one account given by him years after the event had it, a carpenter who worked with him in setting up permanent installations told him of the Director's plan to replace him, immediately after the approaching opening of the exhibit halls, with another anthropologist. Forcing a confirmation with his customary forthrightness and immediacy of action, Boas at once resigned, consenting to remain only long enough to complete the cases he was preparing. A year was to go by before he was to receive another appointment, a year whose problems he never forgot. The experience was to give him deep understanding of the situation of his students who, with almost monotonous regularity in earlier days when posts in anthropology were few in number, experienced similar periods when the future was uncertain for lack of opportunities for professional placement.

Boas joined the American Museum of Natural History in 1896, as assistant curator; in 1901 he was promoted to the rank of curator, which he retained until he severed his connection with the institution in 1905. From this period dates some of his most important work. His paper "The Decorative Art of the Indians of the North Pacific Coast" represents a pioneer analysis of the symbolisms of a non-representational art-form in terms of its own canons of interpretation. The great work on the secret societies and social organization of the Kwakiutl Indians of the same region provided initial insights into the give-away competitions of these people, called the potlatch. These competitons were later to become famous as the exemplification of the theory of conspicuous consumption advanced by Thorstein Veblen—another independent thinker whose work Boas knew but whom he never met, perhaps because of Veblen's shyness, and Boas' inability, lacking the intercession of a formal introduction, to become acquained with those he regarded as his peers. His contributions on the growth of children continued, and his initial paper in mathematical statistics, the first of many to come, entitled "The Cephalic Index," was published. The first of the long series of texts of Indian tales and myths that he had collected and was to continue to collect and publish until his death was brought out as a *Bulletin* of the Bureau of American Ethnology, which, in 1901, appointed him Honorary Philologist.

He also began, during this decade, to look about him at some of the wider problems of the organization of the world of scholarship and the furtherance of scientific research. Such problems came to hold deep meaning for him, and were to bridge the gap between his earlier, more restricted scientific interests and his later concern with national and international policy. In 1889, we find him discussing advances in the methods of teaching anthropology before a meeting of the American Naturalists, and presenting a classification of anthropological data in connection with the International Catalog of Scientific Literature. He was concerned, during the same year, with the Federal Census of 1900, advancing proposals to ensure the proper enumeration of the Indians. 1902 found him emphasizing the need for a national anthropological society to complement local, state and national academies, where the gamut of the sciences was included in a single body. In 1903 he pursued this problem further, treating what has always been, and to the present is one of the vexing difficulties of scholarship, that of finding adequate support for the publication of the results of research.

At this time, too, he advanced practical reasons for studying the cultures of other parts of the world that antedate by almost half a century the development of university programs of area studies. His paper "A Plea for a Great Oriental School" contains passages that might have been written in 1952 in arguing for such programs: "Under present conditions a more extended knowledge of East Asiatic cultures seems to be a matter of great national importance. Our commerce and political intercourse with Eastern Asia are rapidly expanding, and in order to deal intelligently with the problems arising in this area we require a better knowledge of the people and of the countries with which we are dealing. This

is true of China and Japan, and this is true of our Malay possessions." * He had himself furthered this aim in a modest way at
the Museum by making possible the work of Dr. Berthold Laufer,
who later was to become the greatest sinologist of his time, but
who then was still a young man. Yet this, or the professorship of
Chinese that had been established at Columbia, was not enough.
"It would rather seem that what we have to aim at is the gradual
establishment of a department in which all the different cultures
of Eastern Asia are represented, and in which information on the
products, commercial possibilities and social status of these
countries can be imparted." Boas repeated his plea in an address
he gave in April of the same year, but his proposals came to
nothing, and it was not until the press of historic circumstances
made the need for area studies patent to all that the necessary
support was forthcoming for programs of the kind he evisaged
so long ago.

Boas' greatest achievement in research while he was at the
Museum was in the execution by him, and by others working
under his direction, of the various projects undertaken as parts
of the Jesup North Pacific Expedition, conceived to establish the
relationship between aboriginal North America and the tribes of
the Asiatic mainland. It was designed to throw light on some of
the basic theoretical and methodological problems of anthropology—the relation between race, language and culture, the
mode of diffusion of custom, and the ways in which historical relations between nonhistoric peoples, without written records, can
be established. It included archaeological, ethnological, somato-
logical and linguistic studies; its area ranged from British Columbia to the Siberian Arctic.

Boas cast his net widely in obtaining trained personnel to
conduct these researches. It was not too difficult to find anthropologists to study the tribes living on the North American continent, but Siberia was another matter. Boas wrote to the Russian
Academy of Sciences, and this body, after the manner of the time,
recommended two young Russian revolutionists who, from their
exile in Siberia, had been submitting significant reports on the

* The context of this remark indicates that Boas here meant the Philip-
pine Islands.

tribes with which they had been in contact. These two men, Waldemar Bogoras and Waldemar Jochelson, who were to become internationally famous anthropologists, were released from exile to pursue their scientific careers. Jochelson was eventually to die in New York in 1937; Bogoras, honored as an Old Revolutionary, was to remain in Russia until his death in 1936, escaping the purges that, when he was last in Western Europe, in 1930, he foresaw and feared.

The data the Jesup Expedition produced, and the methods it employed, have influenced anthropological thinking in many ways. The somatic and cultural affiliations of the American Indian and the Siberian aborigine are today taken for granted; archaeological research has made steady progress toward documenting the route of aboriginal migration to the Americas across the Behring Straits and the Aleutian Islands. In the broader sense, these field researches, together with the expedition headed by A. C. Haddon, of Cambridge, to the Torres Straits at about the same time, dramatized for anthropologists the need to investigate at first hand the cultures of peoples to be studied, and confirmed the desirability of field investigation as against the "arm-chair" research of the older comparative school. Most important of all, it demonstrated that, given imagination and daring, large-scale, planned attack on a problem, carefully conceived, adequately financed, with its theoretical background well in hand, would yield results of the highest value. Its influence on American anthropology in this respect is reflected in the sustained programs of research on broad problems, over wide areas that have since been initiated in South and Central America, Oceania, Africa, and the Caribbean, utilizing, as Boas did in his pioneer research, historical situations which, in effect, provide the only laboratories where the student of man can obtain adequate scientific control over his complex and elusive data.

The second result of Boas' work at the American Museum of Natural History had to do with arranging specimens for public exhibition. The innovations he made benefit every person who, at any museum in the United States and in many institutions elsewhere in the world, views the ethnographic collections on display. Earlier modes were either haphazard, or on a "comparative" basis, whereby weapons, or clothing, or house-models from all over the world were placed in a single hall, usually in order of their complexity so as to show their "evolution," after the manner of the displays of natural history materials. To Boas, however, this theoretical approach, as we shall see, was untenable, and its results, as concerns the objectives to be attained in showing specimens, undesirable. He was interested, as always, in the ways human beings live. For him, museum specimens were worth exhibiting only because they offered an opportunity to make known the actual modes of life of peoples all over the world.

His point of view was made explicit in a paper published in 1907, wherein he discussed a criticism by George A. Dorsey that the installation of the ethnological collections of the American Museum of Natural History represented "an unsatisfactory attempt at popularizing the results of ethnological research." Dorsey's position was that "the essential object of a large museum must be research, not instruction"; and while Boas granted that "this objective is . . . a legitimate one," he continued, "in addition, there are two other important desirable ends: healthy entertainment and instruction." In developing these points, while Boas showed himself faithful, as ever, to his scientific principles, he is also seen to have been a shrewd psychologist and a realistic analyst. For the visitor seeking entertainment, he urged, materials should be popularized—not by encouraging a slipshod, specious "mastery" of a subject, but by arranging exhibits which bring out "the sublimity of truth and the earnest efforts . . . needed to acquire it." Because of this, "every kind of inaccuracy should be most carefully avoided, and attempts to make all problems appear childish simply by the elimination of everything that is obscure should not be tolerated," while "effectiveness must be based on the effort to concentrate attention, and on the unity of the idea expressed in each exhibit." In popular display no less than when "imparting systematic information," Boas held that effectiveness "does not lie in diversity, but in the thoroughness of the materials presented."

The finest room Boas installed, which best illustrates the principles he later enunciated, was the Northwest Coast hall. His method, here as in the other rooms under his care, was to bring together materials from a given tribe, or groups of tribes having similar cultures, so that the special qualities of their technological and artistic achievement could be sensed even by the most casual visitor. This changed the then conventional static systematic type of display into something that had as dynamic and living a quality as museum specimens can attain, and provided an emotional as well as an intellectual appeal. From this latter point of view, the changes introduced by Boas documented cultural borrowing as an explanation of the fact that peoples living close together manifest greater similarities in their modes of life than those living at a distance. Later, these regional unities were to be given theoretical expression by Clark Wissler, Boas' student and successor at the Museum, when he developed the concept of the culture-area, a concept that has become one of the organizing principles of modern ethnography. Originally applied to the American Indian, it has been used to classify the cultures of Africa, Asia, Madagascar and Oceania, and with the development of area studies its utility has become apparent far outside anthropology. The principles of museum exhibition Boas devised were, over the years, refined and extended—but not superseded—by Nordenskiöld at the Ethnographic Museum in Gothenburg, by Rivet and his associates at the Musée de l'Homme in Paris, to name only two of the many institutions over the world as well as in the United States, small as well as large, where their influence is apparent.

The year Boas assumed his post at the Museum, he was also appointed Lecturer in Physical Anthropology at Columbia University, through the instrumentality of J. Mckeen Cattell, the psychologist. In 1899, the lectureship became a professorship, with permanent tenure, a position Boas held until his retirement in 1937. His connection with the Museum ended in 1905, after a disagreement with the administration. A new period in Boas' life thus once more began. It was marked by no less a degree of ferment than his earlier years; but with his base of operations finally established, Boas was free to consolidate the results he had thus far achieved in building the structure of concept, theory and method that has become such an integral part of anthropology and, through it, of current thought.

6

Boas was forty-seven years old when he left the Museum, to devote himself exclusively to teaching and research. Here he was to develop that small band of students and associates who did so much to make anthropology what it has since become. That this was accomplished during years when anthropology was regarded as something marked by exoticism and amateurishness, starved in the academic curriculum and ignored by those concerned with policy-making and the direction of affairs in the secular world, was in itself a remarkable achievement.

Boas was a formidable teacher. By the undergraduates, his powers were felt rather than appreciated, though during his later years, his classes at Barnard College were popular. Yet to students who were part of a system whereby higher education, as one witty and perceptive observer has remarked, consisted of "swapping points for a degree," his utter lack of concern to academic bookkeeping was baffling. As might be anticipated, they responded in terms of the tradition under which they were obtaining their education, so that only the more mature and more highly motivated of them profited to any degree approaching full measure from what he offered them. When, in 1927, Boas lectured at the New School for Social Research, presenting the materials later incorporated in his book *Anthropology and Modern Life,* the large hall provided for him was crowded by men and women who, it was said, had in the main sat under him as undergraduates, and in their mature years had come to realize their failure to take advantage of the opportunity they had had in college.

Few of the anthropologists Boas trained came from his own undergraduate classes, but rather from other disciplines or other institutions. The quality of his graduate teaching was subtle. Of individual direction, there was almost none. Lectures were not interrupted with questions; these were for "the seminar," the weekly discussion sessions where, each year, a different topic was treated on the basis of student reports. Here Boas was a hard taskmaster, demanding and obtaining the best from the members of the group. Bibliography was assigned, at least in the earlier days, without regard for a student's language competence. If a work in German or Italian or Swedish was relevant, it was the responsibility of the one reporting to find his own means of obtaining the aid he needed to master it.

Since there were no examinations in graduate courses, the student had himself to obtain any knowledge that was a prerequisite for the courses he followed. Boas' indifference to such matters was Olympian. In the famous anthropometry course which, it was held, could not be understood unless taken at least twice, Boas simply assumed the mathematical competence needed to grasp the development of the intricate statistical formulae he employed; in his courses on linguistics, he took an adequate knowledge of technical phonetics similarly for granted. Dissertation topics were brought to Boas for his approval, not suggested by him. Methods employed in obtaining and handling data, and the determination of the manner in which they were to be cast in final form, were the business of the student, to be worked out independently by him; only results were presented for appraisal.

This is undoubtedly one important reason why the term "Boas school" of anthropology, to which reference is sometimes made, is a misnomer. If one considers the contributions of the students whom Boas produced, and of the mature scholars, such as Elsie Clews Parsons, George A. Dorsey and P. E. Goddard, whom he attracted to his circle, one finds the greatest variety of interests, methods and theoretical orientation, whether comparison is drawn between them and Boas himself, or between one another. All Boas' students, however, obtained a sense of the variety of ways in which human behavior can manifest itself, and the need clearly to distinguish what is inherent in the human organism from what is learned.

While Boas granted his students and associates the complete intellectual freedom he demanded for himself, he also held them responsible for what they wrote, and never hesitated to differ with them when he deemed this necessary. It is difficult to know whether he ever fully granted, in his unconscious reactions, that an associate who had once been a student no longer held this relationship to him. It was a sense of something of this sort that gave so many of his ex-students the ambivalences that marked their feeling-tone toward him. He was famous for never commenting on the numerous books and scholarly papers his students wrote, except where there were points of fact or theory he felt should have been treated differently than they were. To those who were less psychologically secure, where the ambivalences were strongest, the absence of any expression of opinion from Boas was painful, and they sometimes took all possible measures to ascertain his reaction to their work. For all of them, however, in time of stress or need, he was a friend on whom they could count for tangible no less than moral support.

One thing Boas did not permit: that anyone speak for him. When, in 1936, A. L. Kroeber attempted to meet criticisms of Boas' work advanced by the South African student Mrs. Hoernle, Boas wrote a "reply" in which, ignoring the original critique, he expounded on his objection to what Kroeber had written of him. "It is interesting to me to read Dr. Kroeber's analysis not only of my scientific work, but also of my personality," he began his "reply." "I may perhaps misinterpret both. Nevertheless, I wish to express my complete disagreement with his interpretation." Or again, when a well-known sociologist, a decade earlier, requested his consent to having one of his more eminent students write a chapter about him in a volume to treat of leaders of social science, he refused in no uncertain terms: "My scientific activities are a matter of public record, and are therefore beyond my control. However, I do not think that the time has yet arrived to write my obituary." Yet it is characteristic of him that to this letter he affixed a few words, written in hand—"P.S. This is not unkindly meant."

CHAPTER TWO

MAN, THE BIOLOGICAL ORGANISM

FOR Boas, the unity of anthropological science was an expression of the conviction that the life of man is itself a unit. It was of course obvious to him that not all students of man could encompass in their studies all aspects of human existence as they are spread out in time and space, or even as they are found within a single society. But for him, it was of first importance that a sense of the underlying unity of man be maintained if the realities of human living were to be grasped, and that the student must be competent to move from one aspect of human life to another in seeking to understand the causalities of human affairs.

Because of his rounded view of the problem, Boas could perceive so clearly the fallacy of eugenist theory, which held the destiny of man to be determined by biological endowment, with little regard for the learned, cultural determinants of behavior. By the same token, however, he refused to accept the counter-dogma that man is born with a completely blank slate, on which can be written whatever is willed. He saw both innate endowment and learning—or, as it was called popularly, heredity and environment—as significant factors in the making of the mature individual.

His stress on the plasticity of the organism in adapting itself to those structured systems of learned behavior termed cultures arose from the need to underscore the fact that culture is learned so well that responses to it are automatic, not inborn; that specific

25

modes of cultural behavior are not the result of innate abilities, instinctively expressed. Racial heredity, Boas repeated over and over, is meaningless. The significant biological factor, for him, was the actual descent line, not the racial category. As he himself phrased it, writing in 1922, ". . . we should distinguish clearly between the hereditary stability of a population and the hereditary characteristics which determine the bodily form and functions of an individual."

The fascination which the study of human physical type held for Boas must in considerable measure have derived from the fact that to this aspect of anthropological science—and, perhaps paradoxically, to linguistics—he could bring his brilliant mathematical talents; that these were the anthropological specialties that approached most closely the discipline of physical science in which he was trained. Unlike most physical anthropologists, he never studied anatomy, though he took care not to overlook requisite anatomical facts in considering the traits he measured. His approach, rather, was anthropometric, utilizing statistical analyses of mass measurements of the living. The emphasis he laid on the dynamics of process in the formation of human types bewildered those committed to the descriptive techniques derived from anatomy, for whom even the computation of simple constants from a small series of skulls presented a problem. It is thus understandable that Boas' work in this field called forth the hostilities, both latent and manifest, which, with comparable loyalties, marked its reception.

Interestingly enough, it was precisely the physical anthropologist who was at the same time a foremost anatomist, T. Wingate Todd of Western Reserve University, who was numbered among Boas' most enthusiastic supporters. Yet despite a degree of productivity in this field alone that would represent the work of a busy lifetime for most scholars, Boas was never elected an officer of the American Association of Physical Anthropologists of which he was a founding member, and its *Journal* carried no obituary notice of him, nor any summary of his work until 1948 when, on the ninetieth anniversary of his birth, an appreciation of his contributions to physical anthropology was published in it, with a bibliography of his titles in the field. By this time, however, the periodical had passed into the hands of a new editor, who did not permit the altercations of a preceding generation to transcend the scientific contributions of those involved.

Boas' first paper in the study of human physical type appeared in 1888. It was a discussion of certain Indian skulls from British Columbia, presented before the New York Academy of Sciences. The time between this and his ultimate writing in this field, an article entitled "Individual, Family, Population and Race," which was posthumously published, almost spans his professional anthropological career. His achievement, in sum, was impressive not only because of the number of studies he made and the bulk of his published reports and analyses, but because his work, despite its deviation from accepted paths, shaped thinking in two major subdivisions of the field, and, in a third, had implications which students, a decade after his death, are only beginning to explore.

These three divisions were the study of the physical growth and development of the child; the problem of the nature of physical difference between human groups, or that of race, with particular reference to the relation between physical type and behavior; and biometrics, with special regard for the unravelling of those processes which have made for the creation of specific local forms, or ecotypes, as Boas sometimes termed them. Yet, though these three aspects of his work can advantageously be considered separately, we must never lose sight of the amount of overlapping between them. Boas' contribution to the area of growth and development of children could not have been made were it not for his ability to develop the statistical techniques essential for the analysis of the problems of child-study that attracted his attenion. The same is also true of his insistence on the essentially statistical character of racial classifications, a point of view that led him to reassess the biological significance of racial differences.

That the work of Boas in this area achieved its marked significance was in no small measure due to the fact that he never permitted the role of tradition in influencing the ultimate form which the physical traits of a given group might assume to be forgotten. Numerous examples can be found, in his reports on the various studies he conducted, of how skillfully Boas was able to weave cultural and biological factors into a single fabric. In 1923, a suit was instituted in the courts of a western state where Orientals were not permitted to own real estate, asserting that Armenians were not Caucasoid, and therefore were not eligible to hold property. Much of the argument turned on the fact that the characteristic "rounded" head of these people, which gave a high ratio of breadth to length (that is, made them extremely brachycephalic), proved their Mongoloid racial affiliation. Boas was retained by the defense as an expert, and at once set to work, with some of his students, measuring the heads of Armenians, who suddenly became most willing subjects.

His approach was typical. He separated those he measured into two categories—persons born in the United States and those who had immigrated. Statistical analysis, even in the preliminary stages of the investigation, showed a significant difference in head-form between the two series. The answer lay in an area far removed from any genetic—that is, racial—consideration. Armenians who had migrated to the United States had the characteristic lack of the occipital protrusion at the back of the head that marked those born in this country, while those native to the United States exhibited this characteristic. In Armenia, children are placed in a cradle-board, on which, after the manner of much of Eastern Europe, they lie on their backs, tightly swaddled. Being unable to toss about, the weight of the head suppresses the development of the occiput; but this genetic trait at once asserts itself in Armenians of American birth who are permitted the free movement that allows unrestricted development of the tender bony structure of the head.

The case was dismissed. For Boas, it had offered another opportunity to demonstrate the complexity of the factors that enter into the formation of the adult physical type, and thus again to caution against a racial approach to the problem of human differences.

2

Racial classification, as such, had slight meaning for Boas. He accepted classification as a step in the scientific analysis of the problem of ascertaining the differences between men, but only as a first step. He early rejected the sanctity of the measurements and indices to which physical anthropologists had come to ascribe intrinsic meaning, yet he defended their employment as a useful technique of investigation. As he wrote in 1899, ". . . The function of measurement is . . . solely that of giving greater accuracy to the vague verbal description. . . . Measurements must be selected in accordance with the problem that we are trying to investigate."

A race was conceived by him as a major grouping of mankind, marked off by genetically rooted physical characteristics that reach far back into antiquity. He considered it a kind of entity whose more widely distributed traits marked an enormous number of specialized local types. When these were stable, they were to be regarded as the result of isolation and inbreeding. If they exhibited a high degree of variability, they were the result of mixture with other types. He always considered race, in any context, in terms of its genetic implications. As he put it in a statement presented to the International Population Congress, meeting in Paris in 1937, "A race must not be identified with a subjectively established type, but must be conceived as a biological unit, as a population derived from a common ancestry and by virtue of its descent endowed with definite biological characteristics."

It is not strange, therefore, that though the racial "scheme" he advanced has often been cited, Boas never regarded it as more than an opinion based on probabilities arising out of our knowledge of the early development of man. Certainly he never gave time to the researches which would have been necessary to validate or revise it. Its simplicity is striking: "Our picture of the principal races would thus be that of two groups . . . inhabiting the shores of the Indian Ocean and of another large group inhabiting the shores of the Pacific Ocean, including both Amer-

icas and a large part of Asia, with the affiliated European type."
That is, for him, the customary system of classifying mankind
into three or four races was to be replaced by a twofold classification—the Negroid, to include the Australoids, and the Mongoloid,
of which the Caucasoid was to be thought of as a sub-type.

Boas' attack on the problem of the differentiation of human
physical types, the basic question for him, was elaborated as a
complex of concepts which, in varying ways, he repeated again
and again. The existing knowledge of prehistoric man did not
make it possible for him to trace the actual course of racial
differentiation, but he held a position, which the materials steadily
being discovered by the palaeoanthropologists support, that the
principal human types represent genetic lines whose stability
justifies the conclusion that the traits which characterize them
were laid down long ago. These types—that is, these races—are,
however, too general to be of use in analyzing the manner in
which differentiation took place. The local variations in physical
type which form an overlay to each of these vast aggregates must
be assigned primary importance, rather than the major divisions
themselves.

To understand such less widely spread differences, comparisons are to be drawn between present populations, not on the
basis of averages alone, but also on that of the inner deviations
that represent the variations of a given trait in a given group. Such
comparisons demonstrate that there is no population which does
not include among its members individuals who, insofar as they
manifest a given trait, cannot be differentiated from some individuals who belong to other groups. The degree of variation
within any of the principal races of man, that is, is greater than
the differences between racial averages. As a corollary, it becomes
apparent that emphasis laid on "racial" differences tends to cause
us to disregard the basic unity of the human physical form.

The processes which Boas held had made for the differentiation of human types were several, but the first two of those Boas
envisaged are the ones which, as we shall see, students of human
genetics later came to take most prominently into account. The
first of these is isolation, which, with its ensuing inbreeding, en-

courages the development of local, specialized types. The second is contact between peoples—the constant mixture of differing types through crossing, a phenomenon whose universality, and whose importance in demonstrating the fact that *homo sapiens* forms one species, Boas never missed the opportunity to stress. But the hypothesis which fascinated him in studying human biology was the one that holds man to be a domesticated animal, partaking of the instability of type and large number of the varieties in form that characterize all domesticated species.

The hypothesis, in somewhat tenuous form, appears initially in his writings in a paper he published in 1894. It was more fully developed in the first edition of *The Mind of Primtive Man,* and further extended in the rewriting of this work in 1938. "This point of view—namely, that the human race in its civilized forms must be compared, not with the forms of wild animals, but rather with those of domesticated animals—seems to me a very important one. . . ." This clause, in both editions, is followed by one which would imply that the phrase "in its civilized forms" was not a major consideration in Boas' thinking: ". . . a somewhat detailed study of the conditions in which various races are found suggests that at the present time, even among the most primitive types of man, changes incident to domestication have taken place almost all over the world." This statement reflects an interesting change from Boas' original acceptance of the findings of Fritsch, which he cited as presumably establishing the fact "that between primitive man and civilized man differences are found which are quite in accord with the differences between wild animals and domesticated animals." In 1911, Fritsch's results are specified as differences in bodily form of South African Bushmen and Hottentots when compared to Europeans, while in 1938, the paragraph which designated those ". . . modern tribes among which the effects of civilization . . . are slight," drops out entirely.

Here we see the insights yielded by Boas' continuous welding of biological to cultural factors. The dynamic elements in domesticating man are entirely cultural, the end-results, that justify placing him in this category are his physical characteristics, genet-

ically determined. The three processes of domestication Boas
indicated in his writing were "change in nutrition and use of the
body," "selection" and "crossing" between different races of the
same species. The cultural character of these, where man is concerned, are patent. Amounts of food and reliability of supply
depend on technological development, while the types of food
consumed are deeply influenced by established food habits of a
people. Fire gives protection against "climate and enemies," thus
enhancing the chances for survival "of varying forms." Selection,
carried on by man where infrahuman domesticated animals are
concerned, is effected by social convention in human groups. Such
traditions as incest prohibitions, exogamy and endogamy, the
killing or nurturing of infants having particular traits, and the
like, shape the differing physical characteristics of men. Finally,
since man comprises a single species, he has mixed his genetic
strains from the earliest days of his existence on earth, producing
perhaps the most thoroughly mongrelized stock of the entire
biological series, and developing new variants through isolation
and inbreeding of the resultant mixtures.

In indicating the analogies between man and the animals
domesticated by man, Boas followed the German scholars, Ranke,
Hahn, Klatt and Fischer, who pointed out that such human traits
as extremely light and dark skin-color, especially the former, are
found only in domesticated animals, and in man. The blue eyes
that characterize certain human types are nonexistent among wild
forms, but are present in horses, dogs, cats, pigs, and other do-
mestic animals. The hair of the poodle, Boas wrote, is analogous
to that of the Negroid; and in class discussions he liked to carry
the analogy further, indicating the resemblance between the soft,
wavy hair of the European and the pelt of the setter, or between
the wiry hair of the Mongoloid and that of the terrier.

The important point for Boas was that the hypothesis of
domestication, in fitting the observed facts, placed the phenomenon of racial differences in a perspective that was also in line
with existing knowledge of the nature of the traits that mark off
human types one from the other. Morphologically, in these terms,
human races cannot be considered of the order of different species,

evolved from different anthropoid forms. To regard these human varieties as being more or less developed, to represent different steps in the evolutionary scale, is thus untenable, since racial differences are only manifestations of earlier mutations preserved under the conditions of domestication. The search for sequences in racial development thus changes its meaning. Social, not natural, selection is the key to understanding the processes of cross-breeding. Together with contact, and inbreeding through isolation, it has produced the human types, superficially different, but in essence similarly formed and endowed, that we call the races of man.

3

Boas himself has summarized his work on growth and development in a chapter entitled "Growth" in his volume of collected papers which consists of a series of excerpts from contributions covering the years 1892–1932. In this chapter, he tells how his attention was drawn to the subject by the work of Bowditch, Peckham and Roberts, which "showed that statures and weights are asymmetrically distributed." Boas was able to demonstrate that this phenomenon, striking at the time in view of prevailing concepts, was caused by the fact that children grow at different rates; or, as it has come to be known to specialists in child development, is an expression of acceleration and retardation.

It is interesting to note, however, that even at the outset of these researches, Boas' interpretations showed how he guarded against possible harmful generalizations. Two years after his initial formulation, Dr. William Townsend Porter, working in St. Louis, published a series of papers, translating his findings concerning variation in height and weight of children into terms of dullness and precocity. "I should prefer," Boas wrote of these conclusions, "to call the less favorably developed grade of children retarded, not dull; these terms are by no means equivalent as a retarded child may develop and become quite bright. . . . Dr. Porter has shown that mental and physical growth are correlated, or depend upon common causes; not that mental development depends upon physical growth."

This was written long before psychological tests gave an instrument that, employed without the excesses in the way of determining presumed "racial" differences in ability, against which Boas unremittingly protested, made reinvestigation of problems such as those raised by Porter subject to more precise analysis. How correct was the assumption of 1895 became clear only after 1941 when, in a paper entitled "The Relation between Physical and Mental Development," he worked out correlations between physical measurements of accelerated and retarded children and their intelligence quotients. These showed, in much more precise terms, that "physical and mental development went hand in hand"—that "the close correlation between anatomical and psychological traits in childhood must be interpreted as due to the influence of the tempo of physiological development over the body and its functions."

Like others concerned with growth of children in the early days of its study, Boas took mass measurements that provided "standard" growth curves for a given population on the basis of averages by age and sex for height and weight. Later, more traits were measured and observed, so as to obtain a more complete picture. This is apparent in the chapter in the Annual Report of the United States Commissioner of Education (for 1904) entitled "Statistics of Growth" written in collaboration with Clark Wissler, which incorporated the results of studies of boys and girls in a number of cities. Such anthropometric dimensions as size of head and face, finger reach, breadth of hand and length of forearm were measured, observations were made of color of hair and eyes, and educational and sociological data such as grade in school and number of brothers and sisters were included. Average increments of growth were computed and plotted, as well as absolute dimensions in the traits studied, the better to envisage the process as a whole. The development of the requisite mathematical formulae was in itself a major contribution. It is not strange that this chapter gave direction to work in the field of child study for many years, and is today one of its acknowledged landmarks.

This, however, was but a beginning, for further problems crowded one another. How does the individual child actually grow? What do repeated measurements of the same children, as against age-for-age averages, reveal as to the manner of their development? What is the relation between acceleration and retardation, on the one hand, and the ultimate character of the physical traits of the adult? Between chronological and physiological age; and how is the latter determined? What is the significance of the increase in average stature of Europeans and Americans? These were the questions that framed long years of measuring, analyzing and testing.

Boas' researches in the field of growth and development flowered in a series of three papers, published in the journal *Human Biology* from 1932 to 1935 under the general title "Studies in Growth," and in another paper presented before the National Academy of Sciences, "The Tempo of Growth of Fraternities." In the former, he brought together much data from the Newark Academy, Horace Mann and Ethical Culture schools and the Hebrew Orphan Asylum of New York City—long series of repeated measurements of the same children. The patterns of growth of individuals were analyzed in relation to stock derivation, or "race," loosely phrased, environmental background and hereditary influences. The relationship between bodily growth and dental development was assessed; the extent to which the phenomenon of increased stature of European populations in recent years was manifest in the offspring of immigrants was explored. The last named paper, on the growth of fraternities, was particularly important. For here Boas demonstrated how acceleration and retardation in the development of the child were basic genetic phenomena; that the patterns of growth are inherited in family lines, with the mode of development of the father tending to be repeated in that of his sons.

The practical implication of his studies in this field was something of which Boas was always aware; their applications were many and of far-reaching impact. The findings of his investigations on the children in the Hebrew Orphan Home considerably influenced orphanage administration. They demonstrated the advantage of a home environment over an institutional one as reflected in the average values for height and weight of children in the orphanage as against orphans placed in foster homes, and thus resulted in the present practice of placing children whose parents are dead or cannot themselves care for their offspring in homes rather than in institutions. The studies he initiated looking toward the determination of physiological age by roentgenographic and other techniques had immediate applicability to the problems of assigning children to proper classes in schools. A government study of bodily size and proportion of children, made so as to facilitate the proper cutting of clothing, enlisted his active interest, aid and advice.

It is not strange that his influence in the field was so great, however. The way he envisaged and phrased problems, and the methods he devised to study them, were such as to appeal both to those whose concern with child development was centered about the scientific problems involved, and to those whose interests were of a more practical nature. Yet, whether occupied with the one approach or the other, Boas always took the long view. His ultimate goal, here as in other phases of his research, was to further the gathering and analysis of fundamental knowledge— in this case, knowledge of the processes of growth that determined the adult form of the human body.

His view, however, caused him to raise questions concerning the mature and senescent individual. To what extent could the major incidents of the life-cycle be predicted from a knowledge of the pattern of growth of early years? What was the nature and timing of the changes that marked the human life-cycle? Should not the study of growth be extended to include the functioning of fully developed traits, and their decay? What was the nature of that process of running down which characterizes the individual life-span, and at what ages were its successive stages manifest? What is meant by death from "normal" causes, and how does the concept of the normality of different causes shift as age increases?

Only a small part of the research program suggested by these questions which, understandably enough, began to appear in Boas' work and writings as he himself grew older, was realized by him. With characteristic ingenuity, and his ability to obtain cooperation for his scientific work from the most unlikely sources, he enlisted the aid of barbers and certain institutions in New York City in a study of the graying of hair. The result of this study, almost the only actual research on the problem of aging he himself undertook or directed, was published in 1932, when he was 74 years old.

Since Boas' death, a new field, called geriatrics, the study of the aged, has been developed. Institutions have been established to investigate the problems of senescence, the nature of the abilities and disabilities which mark the aging. These have been set up as much because of the pressure of changing proportions of young and old on the social system, due to increasing skills of therapeutic and preventive medicine, as the need to solve the purely scientific problems of the whole life-cycle. Yet this also figures, and in it can be seen the working out, with adequate facilities and personnel, some of the questions envisaged and discussed by Boas as he stressed the need for understanding the whole development of man.

4

Boas was a great statistician, yet his concern with actual data caused him always to give precedence to problem over formula. In this he differed from many students of theoretical statistics, whose interest lies in exploring the formulations they develop, leaving the applicability of their findings, and the interpretation of the results obtained from analyzing the facts, to others. Boas was primarily concerned with economy of effort in the light of the mathematical realities and the nature of the materials to be dealt with. Again and again, in his course on biometrics, he would develop the concept of "spurious accuracy." He drove home the point that to carry out an average value or an expression of variability to many decimal places where no more than one, or even none was needed to give the quantity significance, was wasteful and misleading.

He drew a favored example from the work of the intelligence testers. In 1940, in discussing the nature of intelligence in an address delivered before the American Educational Research

Association at St. Louis, he pointed out the difficulties encountered in studying it. "When I speak of the intelligence of a people," he said, "I mean their ability to adapt themselves adequately to the problems of their life." The very term "intellect," he said, is "ill-defined." Phrasing his essentially statistical argument in terms of ordinary discourse, he pointed out that the intellect ". . . cannot be considered a unit, but includes many manifestations of the functions of the nervous system. We have ample evidence that these are dependent upon the structure of the body and when this is true they may be heritable. They share with all other functions the characteristic that they are variable in the individual according to time and circumstance. . . . In so far as intellect is dependent upon structure, it is heritable. In so far as it is a function expressed in behavior, it is variable. The same individual in different situations and in different bodily conditions will show differences in intelligence. Even the basic conditions for which we strive in physiological experiments and which we assume to be present in psychological tests are variable."

In the light of these difficulties, he would point out, it is meaningless to compute with great precision statistical constants showing the averages and the spread of responses to tests held to reveal the degree of intelligence of individuals. What, Boas would rather ask, is the reliability of a given intelligence quotient, in terms of repeated scores made on a test, or on comparable tests, by the same individual? Yet, though critical, he was by no means negative in his reaction to instruments of this type. He severely attacked the statistical procedures employed in presumably ascertaining "racial" differences in intelligence, but when some measure of scientific control could be brought into play, and when tests that were restricted in objective could be employed, he was not averse to using them, as we have already seen.

The amount of anthropometric data he collected or caused to be collected, and which he used in testing his formulae, was immense. There were measurements of Indians of British Columbia, of California, of reservations in the middle west; the effect of race-crossing among the Chippewa was studied. He measured Porto Ricans, Jews, Italians, and Armenians, and drew on data from Sweden, from Bavaria, from Italy and Holland, from

South Africa. His measurements from Toronto, Worcester, New York and elsewhere have been mentioned, and the fact that these not only include observations of large numbers of individuals, but measures of the same traits as manifested in smaller number of children repeatedly studied at different ages. In all instances, however, whatever the study, the research problem always transcended the descriptive level.

His analysis of changes in the head-form of immigrants, as has been stated, was the best-known, and the most controversial research he conducted. This was a stupendous task. A total of 17,821 subjects were measured by Boas and his thirteen assistants. The results, summarized in a partial report, but most succinctly presented in a paper Boas published in 1912 in the *American Anthropologist* under the title "Changes in Bodily Form of Descendants of Immigrants," created a sensation. For the first time in an anthropometric research program, large numbers of families were studied to permit hereditary influence to be held as constant as possible in the subsequent analysis of the play of environmental factors on physical type. The biometric techniques of study were strange and bewildering to conventional students of the physical form of man. Head-form was the trait most beloved of those who were concerned with the question of racial differences, the problem that occupied most physical anthropologists of the time. The stability of head-form in a population, however, had been taken for granted, as it had to be unless numerous conclusions that had been based on its use were to be questioned. Yet this trait was shown by the results to be anything but stable—responsive, rather, to environmental influences.

The challenge to current biological thought was even more far-reaching. At that time, the doctrine of the autonomy of genetic determinants of physical type received almost unquestioned acceptance. Yet in this study, children of long-headed Sicilian immigrants, born in the United States, were shown to be less dolichocephalic than their parents; while the same phenomenon, in reverse, was found to be manifest among the short-headed, brachycephalic East European Jews and their offspring. More than this, the study showed that the longer the time between the arrival of parents in the United States and the birth of a child, the greater the average deviation in cephalic index of the off-spring from the parental average. Such results could not but argue for the immediate effect of environmental factors on physical type, of a kind and to a degree held impossible by the biologists and physical anthropologists of the day.

Boas fought a valiant battle in support of his position. Where his critics were competent, and their points phrased in accordance with the conventions of scientific discussion, he replied in kind. But where he felt that controversy arose out of bias and lacked technical competence, his answers could be searing. "I must apologize to anthropologists familiar with the methods of anthropometry for the space taken by a discussion of the criticisms by Mr. Radosavljevich, . . . in which the author assumes the pose of an expert, with what right will appear from the following remarks. Since the *American Anthropologist* submits contributions before acceptance to the judgment of authorities, and since, nevertheless, the article has found its way into the journal, it would seem that a discussion of certain elementary facts of anthropometrical method may be useful not alone to the reader unfamiliar with the subject." In the same paper, he replied to the criticism that his study would "destroy the whole value of anthropometry, in particular that the cephalic index has been shown to have no importance." "On the contrary," he asserted, his results ". . . have merely demonstrated that . . . the anthropometric method is a most important means of elucidating the early history of mankind and the effect of social and geographical environment upon man."

Other answers were published in organs of more general circulation, as well as in anthropological periodicals. In 1928 Boas brought out his volume entitled *Materials for the Study of Inheritance in Man*, wherein he presented the raw data of his research, so that all might have them available for analysis. The book, with its one page of text followed by the interminable figures that represent the measurements for each subject in every trait studied, stands as a monument to Boas' scientific integrity, his willingness to allow the results of a major piece of research to be judged on the basis of the facts.

But Boas, over the years, argued in vain. Indeed, a detailed analysis of the reactions to this study, if it is ever made, will comprise an enlightening chapter in the intellectual history of our time. Objections were raised that the differences in observational error of Boas' assistants, given in a table in the original report, were serious enough to invalidate the results. It was asserted that comparisons between parents and their own children was inadmissible because of the small number of cases; that the individuals measured were not of pure descent; that the findings resulted from a process of biological selection rather than environmental influences. Few, apparently, as the years went on, troubled to read the disclaimers and the delimitations of the study set forth by Boas himself in the reports of the work. And few defenders appeared; for what "defense," indeed, was possible, other than repetition of the enormous project by some other student, working independently? And though Boas protested this was the only means of checking his work, none of his critics attempted to document their arguments with fresh, independent data.

The cumulative effect of criticism was irresistible, and today in various works on sociology, population problems and the like one still encounters statements to the effect that, "Franz Boas made an extended study of the effect of immigration to the United States on the head-form of immigrants, concluding that the American environment was producing a new physical type. This conclusion has since been shown to be false." Nothing, of course, could be further from the truth than such an interpretation of the results of this study. Actually, Boas was never convinced that the fact that these changes occurred in the United States was in itself significant. In discussing this research, he often commented on the results comparable to his own from a study conducted in Bavaria by Ammon, which showed the inhabitants of Munich to be less long-headed than in the surrounding country. Ammon attributed this to social selection, taking the position that longer-headedness was associated with greater initiative and higher capacity than shorter-headedness. Boas, rejecting this interpretation on the basis of the evidence, turned to the environmental factor of city as against country life to explain the comparability of the results he had found in New York with those of Ammon on the Müncheners.

If Boas did not yield his position, he likewise refused to rest content with his results. Some years later found him working in Porto Rico, where he determined that the head-form of the present inhabitants exhibited an average increase of five units over the Spanish average, "an increase . . . which can in no way be accounted for by genetic considerations." He set two of his students to measuring second generation Sicilians in New York and Philadelphia, where the results suggested that the process of head-shortening found earlier was intensified in the next generation, or, as Boas conservatively put it, "the result of the two series agreed with those obtained previously." Research on Boston Jews that, though restricted in scope, produced findings in accord with those of the larger study; studies among Mexican immigrants and in Hawaii, have still further strengthened the presumption of the validity of the original conclusions.

Whatever the causes operative in these cases, the principles of "great plasticity of human types" that Boas emphasized in pointing the significance of the head-form study, and that "permanence of types in new surroundings appears rather as the exception than as the rule" he felt he had established, have come to be widely accepted. And herein lies the most significant discovery of the study, the "instability" of the human form, as Boas termed it. On this basis, one need but postulate that the human organism inherits a series of limits within which traits may vary with differing environmental conditions, rather than a number of fixed traits, and the difficulty is resolved. And with its resolution, another of the dichotomies, that of heredity *versus* environment, which has caused so much controversy, falls into its proper place, with its terms not those of irreconcilable opposites, but of complementary forces in shaping the organism.

5

There is considerable reason to believe that, with the years, the most important contribution of Boas to the study of anthropometry and human genetics will turn out to be described by the formula:

$$\sigma_{pop} = \sqrt{\sigma^2_{fam} + \sigma^2_{fr}}$$

This formula, which expresses the fact that the gross variation of a given population has two components, the average differences between its families plus the average variability within these families, subsumes the results of his long study of the role of descent lines in determining the character of a population. It represents a method that, however phrased, we have come to understand must in some way be employed if a dynamic, rather than a static, classificatory approach to the analysis of human physical type is to be had.

In making his study of immigrants, he felt the need to develop a method which would permit him to break down the variability of a given population in a given trait into the genetically determined sub-variabilities which make up the total variation that alone was customarily indicated. It was not until 1916 that he achieved his initial mathematical formulation and proofs, and had worked through the data which furnished materials with which to put his postulates to the test. At that time he published his first paper on the subject, entitled "On the Variety of Lines of Descent Represented in a Population." Here the position was that represented in the formula given above, though the mathematical handling was more complex than in after-years, when further testing brought refinement and simplification.

At a distance of several decades, one must go to the anthropological periodicals of the time this paper appeared to understand how striking a departure it was from the customary ways of handling data. Where physical anthropologists of that day did not concern themselves with the detailed description of the dimensions of a single skull, they recorded the measurements of a small series of adults, usually males, drew a simple average, and phrased their conclusions as to the racial affiliation of the people studied. It was a time when Deniker's *Races of Man* and Ripley's *Races of Europe* represented the typical scientific approach to the study of human physical form. Biometrics was a rudimentary discipline. Galton's influence was beginning to be felt—in Boas' own work, for example—but its real impact came with the publications of Galton's disciple, Karl Pearson and Pearson's followers, in the journal *Biometrika*. The rediscovery of the Mendelian formula for studying heredity had been made a decade and a half previously, but the problems and complexities of genetics that came with the continued probing of later years were unrealized.

It is not, actually, too far-fetched to compare the fate of Boas' paper to that of Mendel's original formulation. This, it will be remembered—for it is one of the favorite tales in the history of science—though published in a reputable zoological journal of world-wide circulation, fell for want of any established body of interest in the problem that would cause biologists to consider, discuss, and further assess in their research the propositions he advanced. In the biology of 1865, as in the physical anthropology of 1915, the primary aim was description and classification, not the study of dynamic processes. The analogy between Boas' paper and that of Mendel becomes more striking when it is realized that it took about the same period of time, some thirty-five years, for their respective professions to reach the point in orientation toward dynamics these students had earlier reached.

Here, however, the comparison ends. For if Mendel's work furnished the basis for later studies in genetics, it has been these developments in genetics and biological "systematics," not Boas' attack on the question of human heredity, that have stimulated the studies in this field that mark the physical anthropology of 1950 and later. It was from these sources, not the principle of family and fraternal variation, that the physical anthropologists have come to the concept of the "breeding isolate," developed by students of heredity to aid in assessing the role of opportunity for contact between individuals and groups as a factor in promoting or inhibiting genetic change in a given species or subspecific type.

This is a useful concept, and with reworking to meet the needs of human biology should yield fertile results. In basic concept, it differs but little from Boas' idea of the population as the unit for study—the population with its traditions of assortative or free mating as instruments in the determination of its physical type. The physical anthropologists, however, have done something Boas did not do. They have taken over the hypothesis of the "breeding isolate" from the animal geneticists without serious modification, which is why its treatment as concerns man has tended to remain theoretical, deductive and undocumented. Based on assumptions concerning the presumed character and rate of change in the genetic composition of inbred or cross-bred populations, discussions of it are phrased in terms of the "evolution" of human types; and, as concerns time, of decades or centuries, as against the millennia with which the latter-day student of biological evolution deals in studying the origin of species.

The factor of tradition, which Boas handled with such sureness, is falteringly employed. This is understandable, for no theory taken over from the students of infrahuman, non-culture building forms can be expected to take the element of culture adequately into account. This, perhaps, is why the proponents of the promising field of human genetics are calling for studies, by students of culture, of differing marriage customs and mating habits, despite the many such studies already made, to aid them in establishing the consequent genetic drift to be expected on the basis of their theoretical propositions, in the relevant societies. This means that the physical anthropologists are being forced by the nature of their new approach to include in their calculations the fact, basic in Boas' research, that the critical element in the breeding habits of man is cultural—that the traditions of a people concerning the desirability of a given type as a spouse, or the social conventions governing marriage in a community, in the final analysis, determine who will mate with whom. It needs only the resumption of measuring entire families, computing the family and fraternal variabilities, and checking these against mating habits and the results which would be expected of the breeding isolate under investigation to complete the circle. This done, the insights in the approach to the dynamics of change in population type initiated by Boas in his study of family and fraternal variability will be enlarged and informed by adding to it the analysis of the genetic processes whereby human types have been differentiated and consolidated into existing forms.

CHAPTER THREE

MAN, THE CULTURE-BUILDING ANIMAL

IT is illuminating to contrast Boas' contribution to ethnology with the role he played in physical anthropology. In the latter, as we have seen, he was the supreme theorist as well as the resourceful and careful methodologist, an innovator who pointed new paths and beat them out for others to follow. In the study of culture, however, though he was always the critical thinker, and despite the enormous influence he had on the development of the subject, the discoveries to be attributed to him cannot be as sharply delimited as those made by him in his study of children, or concerning the relation between heredity and environment, or of the importance of the family line in determining physical type. The reason for the different roles he played in physical and cultural anthropology is twofold. It lies, first, in the nature of Boas' talents and his mental set, as this determined his approach to scientific problems, and secondly in the status of the study of culture at the time he entered it.

In physical anthropology the data manifest a degree of regularity in structure and functioning that make them susceptible to precise analysis. The variables are comparatively restricted, and can in any event be manipulated, statistically and conceptually, if not experimentally. They furnish materials which were congenial to Boas' early training, and to which, as has been pointed out, he could bring his gifts as a mathematician.

In contrast, a culture presents to the student a phenomenon

of kaleidoscopic quality, having variables seemingly endless in number where, certainly in the study of peoples without written history, scientific controls are always tenuous and at best hypothetical. It is not a matter of the difference between the methods of natural science and the historical approach. Language, which can be analyzed with as much precision as any natural phenomenon, is a part of culture, seemingly as arbitrarily fashioned as any other cultural aspect. As spoken by a people, its patterning no more enters into conscious thought than do the patterns of culture in general. But how, other than in descriptive terms, is one to analyze with comparable preciseness a religion, a code of ethics, an economy?

It is significant that one of the aspects of ethnology that intrigued Boas was the study of kinship systems, as they are to be abstracted from the terms of relationship used by a people. Here the problems of inducting generalizations from the observed facts, and the ordering of the data in terms of their inner relations, constituted the kind of a challenge to which he could, in his own terms, give effective scientific response. Traditionally no phase of the study of social organization is more deeply rooted in anthropological practice than this. In conventional hands, it had come to be what one member of the profession termed "the bastard calculus of anthropology," but Boas' attack was independent and unconventional. The diagrams he drew were, from the point of view of customary treatment of the subject, strange indeed. What he did, and what he taught his students, several of whom made noteworthy contributions to the study of kinship, was never to permit the conventions to dominate the data, but to shape diagrams so as to show most clearly the nature of the system, and what it did in ordering the behavior of those who lived in accordance with it.

His paper on Kwakiutl social organization, published in 1920, shows this clearly; shortly thereafter his analysis of the kinship system of the Vandau of Portuguese East Africa appeared as even a more striking example of his ability to cut through form to reach underlying meaning. On the basis of data gathered from a Mundau who was studying at Columbia, he worked out the principles of this complex structure, which is based on the importance of generation, and derives its rationale from the fact that since a woman's brother becomes head of the family when his sister marries, he controls her choice of a mate. Hence in this system, the apparently curious device whereby a woman "descends" one generation when she marries, becoming the equivalent of her brother's child, her children becoming his "grandchildren" and calling him by the reciprocal of that term, when analyzed reveals a whole series of social and economic relationships that would otherwise be inexplicable. By following the data, rather than compressing them into a preconceived framework, their basic organizing and validating principles became apparent, and the working of the kinship structure as a whole could be readily discerned.

The second reason for the difference in the quality of Boas' contribution to physical anthropology and to ethnology, the status of these branches of anthropology during his professional career, is the more important of the two. Physical anthropology, in its conventional form, during the whole of Boas' lifetime, made the collection of data the first charge on its efforts, and beyond this aimed at little more than using these data to classify human groups into races. In terms of categories of scientific procedure, its work lodged on the essentially primary levels of description and classification. The protest of one industrious and respected measurer of bones, when asked what use he made of the data he set down, is not atypical. "It is not for us to do more than record the facts as carefully as we can," he replied. "Sooner or later someone will come who will put them to use."

The inquiring mind was thus, in a very real sense, free to reach out after answers to fundamental questions, to devise new methods of attacking the problems of scientific analysis they posed. The theory that cultural behavior was the result of racial determinism, as it is called, manifests the weakness under analysis that any simplistic explanation of a complex phenomenon shows. Controversies over the race or sub-race to which a given type was to be assigned, on the basis of whether blue eyes or wiry hair or a given form of the head or nose were present, offered little challenge to a resourceful thinker. And while Boas devoted a great deal of energy to combatting racial determinism, especially in the later years of his life, this meant in essence no more than utilizing the results of scientific research in arguing political and social controversy.

In ethnology, on the other hand, some of the most fertile minds in the world community of intellectual endeavor, as it existed during the early years of Boas' professional career, had speculated on the reasons for the similarities and differences to be discerned in the ways of life of peoples with diverse cultures, on the origin and mode of development of their customs, and the reasons why they maintained older forms of thought and behavior or had been hospitable to new ones. We need only name such figures as E. B. Tylor and Herbert Spencer in England, of Lewis H. Morgan in the United States, of Adolf Bastian, Wilhelm Wundt and Friederich Ratzel in Germany, of Auguste Comte and Emile Durkheim in France, to say nothing of many lesser luminaries, to make the point. One might differ with such men on theoretical, conceptual or methodological grounds, but one could not differ with them without deeply respecting the quality of mind that had produced the ideas they advanced.

Boas, who was to be instrumental in the ultimate rejection of some of their ideas, and the revision of others, had no lack of appreciation for the work of those he opposed, especially in the case of the earlier giants of ethnology. To them he paid his tribute again and again, writing in terms such as these: "Anthropology owes its very existence to the stimulus given by these scholars and to the conclusions reached by them. What had been a chaos of facts appeared now marshalled in orderly array, and the great steps in the slow advance from savagery to civilization were drawn for the first time with a firm hand. We cannot overestimate the influence of the bold generalizations made by these pioneers of modern anthropology. They applied with vigor and unswerving courage the new principles of historical evolution to all the phenomena of civilized life, and in doing so sowed the seeds of the anthropological spirit in the minds of historians and philosophers. Anthropology, which was hardly beginning to be a science, ceased at the same time to lose its character of being a single science, but became a method applicable to all the mental sciences and indispensable to them."

This passage is of particular interest, not only in showing Boas' attitude toward those with whom he differed, but also in assessing his own position. It reveals his work as anchored firmly in the past of his discipline, thus to profit from the sense of historical continuity that marked all his thinking, and on which he laid particular stress in evaluating the position of others. It also shows his conception of the study of culture as a "mental" science, which, as we shall later see, with his historical approach to cultural dynamics, constitutes the primary facets of his positive contribution to ethnological theory. But, most important of all, the final statement indicates the level on which he was to make his most telling attacks on the theories of culture current in his day. Even in 1904, when the passage quoted above was written, he could foresee the area in which anthropology was to make its broadest contribution to scholarship and to have its greatest impact on the thought of the years to come.

For time has proved Boas correct in this, as in so many other assumptions he made at various stages in his career. The term "cross-cultural approach" came into vogue after his death. In all probability, given his conservatism where terminology was involved, he would not have liked it had he known it. But as it has come to be used, it actually comprehends, in a phrase, what is implied in the final sentence of the passage of the address Boas delivered in 1904. The knowledge of how to grasp the meaning and values of ways of life other than one's own has opened new vistas for research and theoretical orientation to all the disciplines that study man, whether they be thought of as social sciences or humanistic in nature. More than this, in the field of world politics, the cross-cultural point of view lies at the base of the developing philosophy of cultural relativism, a position inescapable in the light of the study of the diverse inner drives which motivate human thought and channel cultural behavior in different societies.

2

The dominant theory of ethnology at the time Boas entered anthropology was that culture—or society, as it was variously phrased—had evolved, and was evolving from simple to complex forms, from lower to higher modes of life. It was, like all theories, a product of its times. It is commonly assumed to have been an offshoot of the Darwinian hypothesis; but it rather came as a parallel development, a consequence of the differing application of a general point of view, a *Zeitgeist*, so to speak, by scholars who were concerned with different aspects of the world about them. This has been clearly demonstrated by Frederick J. Teggart, the historian; and it is strange that Boas, who must have known his writings, never indicated his cognizance of this fact, even in discussions of anthropological history he wrote after Teggart's work appeared.

Evolutionism arose with the expanding universe of knowledge in Europe, when the conquest of the nonliterate world afforded what was accepted as proof positive of the cultural superiority of the peoples who had devised the means to impose their rule on the diverse societies that the voyages of the preceding four centuries had discovered. It was a heady time, with no place for doubts as to ethnocentric values. Progress, not degeneration, was the word; and the apex of progress was in Europe and, for some, in the American offshoot of European civilization as well. In the view of Lewis H. Morgan, "The hypothesis of human degradation to explain the existence of barbarians and savages, who were found, physically and mentally, too far below the conceived standard of a supposed original man . . . was never a scientific proposition supported by facts."

The theory of cultural evolution was strong in its logic, weak in its method, and this was the point of the attack through which it eventually succumbed. How much its methodological deficiencies were due to the fact that it was an article of faith is to be seen in Tylor's summary dismissal of the way in which a "means of measurement" of the degree of evolution a society had achieved might be determined. "The educated world of Europe and America," he said, "practically settles a standard by simply placing its own nations at one end of the social series and savage tribes at the other, arranging the rest of mankind between these limits according as they correspond more closely to savage or to cultured life." Other students of the period did attempt more precisely to order the degree of development of various societies, or, more often, of the various stages they assumed had marked the evolution of religion, or family organization, or art or political structure, but their essential point of view was not much different from this.

The classical term for the doctrine that comprehended the basic assumption of the evolutionists is called "the psychic unity of man." It is a difficult hypothesis, requiring much refinement and clarification before it can become a useful scientific instrument, and has continued under examination. It was not solely employed by the English students of culture of the evolutionary school. The German anthropologist Bastian had developed the concept of the basic ideas, the *Elementargedanken* that are found in all cultures, and make for what, in Boas' words, Bastian demonstrated to be the "appalling monotony of the fundamental ideas of mankind all over the globe." The geographers, in postulating the similar response of man to analogous natural settings, also employed this unity as an essential element in their argument.

Since the postulate of the psychic unity of man was systematically used by the evolutionists, Boas was expressing the realities of the history of anthropology when, in 1904, he sketched the nature and place of the concept. "The evolutionary idea," he pointed out, "was based essentially on the observation of the sameness of cultural traits the world over. On the one hand, the sameness was assumed as proof of a regular, uniform evolution. On the other hand, it was assumed to represent the elementary idea which arises by necessity in the mind of man and which can not be analyzed, or as the earliest surviving form of human thought." Or, as he had put it eight years previously, "while formerly identities or similarities of culture were considered incontrovertible proof of historical connection, or even of common origin," they were now interpreted as "results of the uniform working of the human mind."

For Boas, as for others of his time and since, the doctrine of the psychic unity of man held, as it holds, an ambiguous quality. In essence, it stresses the similarities in the cultures man has erected—which undoubtedly exist—but tends to neglect the unique local and regional developments that also exist, and make of each way of life the particular kind of entity it is. Always, in discussing the problem, the explanation in biological terms must be taken into account. Is man one, or do his racial differences make him many? Cannot the differences between cultures be referred to the particular abilities of the peoples who live in accordance with them? If man is one, that is, why are cultures different?

The position of the early students of culture who stressed the psychic unity of mankind followed its own logic. As Boas phrased it in *The Mind of Primitive Man,* and emphasized in his lectures: "The similarity of fundamental customs and beliefs the world over, without regard to race and environment, is so general that race appeared to them as irrelevant. . . . We do not find in their writings any mention of racial differences." What, however, of the special manifestations of this human trait of creating culture found in different parts of the world, when we regard these as an overlay to the similarities that lie beneath them?

The answer, quite different from that given by those who held for the classical doctrine of the psychic unity of man, has come to be so accepted by students of man that it is no longer debated. It can be well described by quoting further from the paragraph where the statement of Boas just cited is found: "The psychological basis of cultural traits is identical among all races, and similar forms develop among all of them. . . . The whole problem of the development of culture is therefore reduced to the study of psychological and social conditions which are common to mankind as a whole, and to the effect of historical happenings and of natural and cultural environment." Cultural similarities, that is, arise from the needs of man and out of his earliest historical experience; the differences between cultures are the result of reactions to the differing historic and geographical forces with which different human groups and their ancestors had to deal.

For the early students who held for the psychic unity of man, however, the concept was far less flexible than this. The evolutionists conceived of it as the expression of human capacity to develop culture in accordance with a set sequence of stages, without reference to time or place. This took specific terms—from sexual promiscuity to monogamy, from food-gathering to agriculture, from animism to monotheism, from pictorial to non-representational art. They did not hold that the psychological unity of man was to be discerned in his potential to create cultures having certain broad resemblances. They rather believed that it manifested itself in a specific series of human abilities that would drive a group, if left to itself, up the ladder of progress, through ever higher stages of evolution, eventually to reach the attainments of the civilizations of Europe and America.

Boas parted company with the evolutionists, whose concept of man as one he accepted, on the issue of methodology. He tersely summarized his position in 1920, after the battle had been won: "As soon as we admit that the hypothesis of a uniform evolution has to be proved before it can be accepted, the whole structure loses its foundation. . . . If we admit that there may be different ultimate and coexisting types of civilization, the hypothesis of one single general line of development cannot be maintained." Obviously the only factual proof of cultural evolution—as against the fact of cultural change—can be provided by the archaeological record. But this is precisely the one source where adequate evidence cannot be secured, except as regards that relatively small part of culture consisting of material objects that have been preserved in the earth—tools, weapons, and in later periods, housing, clothing, and graphic and plastic art. The nature of the family, the character of the political structure, the concept of the universe, the songs sung or the tales recounted in early days are gone beyond recall. Only by inference can we in any degree grasp their primary forms, and even then no objective proofs of the correctness of our inferences can be produced.

It is, however, pointless to argue along this line when discussing the position of the classical evolutionists. They rarely made reference to the factual data from early man, any more than did those who opposed them, including Boas and the students who followed him. The argument on both sides was on the level almost of pure theory. For the comparative method, as the technique used by the evolutionists in making their point regarding the psychic unity of mankind and the inevitability of the evolutionary progression was called, in its classical form entailed much more than drawing comparisons between data held to be similar. This is continually done in anthropological research, as when the distribution of elements in cultures without writing is mapped, for example, so that historic contacts can be reconstructed; or, where written history is available, when comparisons are made to enable us to understand how a given cultural element has changed form and meaning in a new setting. Granting the classical concept of the psychic unity of man, however, whereby all cultural phenomena must result from the operation of the same causes, the factors of time depth, spatial relationships and psychological significance could be, and were, disregarded. If one wished to know the line of development of a given institution, following Tylor's prescription, the data would be arranged without reference to these factors on a subjectively determined developmental scale, and the resulting demonstration sufficed.

But though the demonstration was logically satisfactory, the method which produced the presumed proofs was not. As Boas observed in 1896, "We find many types of structure of family. It can be proved that paternal families have often developed from maternal ones. If we do not make the assumption that the same phenomena have everywhere developed from the same causes, then we may just as well conclude that paternal families have in some cases arisen from maternal institutions, in other cases in other ways." Or, as he phrased it earlier the same year, in reviewing A. F. Chamberlain's book, *The Child and Childhood in Folk-Thought*, "The object of anthropological research being to elucidate psychological laws on the one hand and to investigate the history of human culture on the other, we must consider it a primary requirement that only such phenomena are compared as

are derived psychologically or historically from common causes.
. . . Only the common mistake of attributing any two phenomena that are somewhat alike to a common cause can explain
the reasoning that led the author to amass and to place side by
side entirely heterogeneous material."

To think in simple terms of so complex a phenomenon as
culture, to regard only one possibility in many alternative lines of
development of an institution as valid, was for Boas indefensible.
Again and again, he adduced proofs of multiple causation. Archaeology was one of the anthropological specialties where he
did little work, but one use he made of archaeological data was
to afford a striking instance of what happens when the actual
facts of a specific cultural sequence are brought to bear on a
theory of universal stages assumed to mark the evolution of a
particular aspect of culture; in this case, of decorative art. It will
be remembered that here two points of view were debated. One
held that realistic art-forms had evolved out of geometric designs,
the other that pictorial art came first, and broke down into ab-
stract decorative compositions. In Mexico, in an actual series of
strata, pots, decorated with a realistic fish-like design, were shown
to have degenerated under mass production into a series of meaningless geometric motifs, which in turn were reinterpreted into a
composition that was again realistic, but where, instead of fish,
leaves were depicted.

Certain philosophical aspects of evolutionism, that involved
the drawing of value-judgments, presented difficulties of a different kind and, as we shall later see, were rationalized rather
than resolved. But where objective proofs could be employed to
test hypotheses, the demonstrations grew more convincing as
Boas and later some of his students marshalled the evidence that
led to the ultimate replacement of the theory of unilinear evolution by postulates susceptible of testing by reference to the facts.

Boas' critique of evolutionism, and such concepts as that of
convergence, which grew out of this critique, stand as major
contributions to anthropological theory. The methodology employed in the attack was likewise an important gain; it has met
the test of time, and its principles have become commonplace in

anthropological science. In the same way, his assertion of cultural pluralism, that to envisage "different ultimate and coexisting types of civilization" is more reasonable than to think of the human story as a unilineal development to a single socio-cultural end, desirable above all others, has forced its acceptance by the sheer weight of the ethnographic and archaeological materials that have been collected since he wrote these words.

So completely did Boas make his case, indeed, that no serious question was raised during the latter years of his life as to the validity of his position. Only after his death did an eddy of neo-evolutionism appear in the stream of Euroamerican anthropological thought. Reasoning from an assumed primacy of technology in determining other forms of custom, and employing the data of prehistory where technological developments can in some measure be traced, the neo-evolutionists have attempted to resuscitate the comparative method and, by inference, the classical principle of psychic unity on which it rested. Some who take this position discuss their propositions calmly on the basis of the available data; in other instances, however, the attacks leveled against Boas have been bitter, and couched in terms of recrimination that he himself, in discussing the position of the earlier evolutionists with whom he differed, never employed. The Russian anthropologists have also come to reject Boas' position regarding cultural and social evolution, since his scientific eclecticism does not lend itself to conformity with politically established dogma.

3

In 1907, Boas delivered a lecture at Columbia University bearing the simple title "Anthropology." After analyzing the evolutionist position, he went on to discuss "an entirely new view regarding the relation of the races" which developed when "attempts were made to fit the hypothetical typical evolution of mankind to the historical development of culture in different parts of the world, so far as it had been reconstructed." These attempts, he pointed out, showed increasingly that "the theory was hardly ever applicable to specific cases"; how even "in prehistoric times transmission of cultural elements has been almost unlimited, and that the distances over which inventions and ideas have been carried cover whole continents."

This "new view" was the theory of diffusion. It was not as new as Boas' phrase might imply, nor was his discussion of it in any sense the announcement of a discovery of his own. The scholars who espoused the evolutionary position did not deny that ideal sequences could be invaded should a people in a "lower" stage of culture take over techniques or ideas from those presumably more highly developed than they. Tylor, in particular, had recognized the importance of cultural borrowing. None of the evolutionists, however, had gone as far as Boas in asserting that, because of "cultural transmission," as he termed it, "the culture of any given tribe, no matter how primitive it may be, can be fully explained only when we take into consideration its . . . relation to the culture of its near and distant neighbors and the effect that they may have exerted."

Diffusionism, like any theory that represents the swing of a pendulum from an extreme position, tended to generate enthusiasms that exceeded the mandate given by data and method. These enthusiasts appeared in two countries. In Germany, Fritz Graebner and W. Foy of the ethnological museum of Cologne, founded what came to be known as the culture-historical school. In England, Sir Grafton Elliot Smith and his disciple, W. E. Perry, took the position that man, after spreading his humble hunting and food-gathering cultures over the earth, had achieved "civilization" in Egypt alone, so that all other "higher" cultures, such as those of India, Mexico and Peru, derived from the diffusion of Egyptian custom.

Boas recognized the validity of the principle of diffusion, but in terms of a controlled methodology; selectively, as he approached all theory. It must be remembered that though he had opposed the evolutionists, he could also write that "much of the older theory seems plausible." Thus the idea of the basic unity of mankind, which he accepted in revised form, led him to regard it as one explanation of the consequent limitation of possibilities of invention, a concept which he developed to explain why peoples living in widely different parts of the world might independently create the remarkably similar elements to be observed in their cultures. But while he agreed that any people will take over cultural items from others, and that this is an important mechanism in the development of human civilization, he insisted that the problem of diffusion must be studied in specific regions, where the assumption of historic contact between peoples manifesting similarities in their customs must be strong enough to justify the hypothesis of transmission.

Boas thus approached the question of the historic contact between nonliterate societies, the task of reconstructing history which again and again he emphasized was the basic problem of anthropology, with his customary empiricism. The Jesup Expedition, which, it will be remembered, was planned to study the relationship between the peoples of the American Northwest and Siberia, and executed years before the controversy over diffusion began, had as one of its stated aims, "The investigation of the languages and cultures of the coast tribes with particular reference to the question of the dissemination of culture." Years later it was his students who, analogously, traced the details of the Sun Dance among different Plains Indian tribes to ascertain with precision what elements of this complex rite were found in what cultures; studies which enabled them to draw conclusions not only as to what had been diffused, but how the elements that moved from tribe to tribe had been adapted and readapted in each new setting.

The diffusionist fantasies of Elliot Smith received scant attention from Boas. His theory was discussed in classes and seminars, but its excesses were so patent that it needed little more than exposition to lay bare its weaknesses. In this, Boas was not alone. Though the strident polemics of the leader of this heliolithic school caused most of those who differed with him, especially in England, to stay out of range of the cudgel with which he lay about him, the incisive attack on his position in the Frazer lecture delivered by R. R. Marett in 1927, on "The Diffusion of Culture," was enough to cause the collapse of the overinflated structure. The avocation of tracing about the world the distribu-

tion of gold and pearls used as valuables, of megalithic monu-
ments and pyramids, of the practice of mummification, and of
rulers regarded as children of the sun, presented too many historical and methodological difficulties to merit serious consideration. True, it had afforded the framework for one of the early
best-selling popularizations of science, H. G. Wells' *Outline of
History,* but this work, like most others of its kind, was written by
one outside the field; and anthropologists, like historians, regarded it with the tolerance of the professional for the amateur,
when they read it at all. Elliot Smith, a great anatomist, was in
ethnology a tyro; and the fate of his ethnological "discovery" was
an earnest of the degree to which the science had grown since the
days of its domination by the amateur and the antiquarian.

Graebner and the *Kulturehistorische Schule* were, however,
quite another matter. Here were no novices, but trained professionals. Graebner himself was a museum curator, a man who had
thought deeply about the basic theoretical and methodological
implications of the study of culture. The slight volume in which
he presented his ideas, his *Methode der Ethnologie,* was backed
by substantial contributions to leading anthropological journals,
where his position was documented by an array of factual materials. The theory, moreover, attracted, held, and has continued
to attract many competent scholars. Largely because of the criticisms raised against it by Boas and his students, it never gained
acceptance in the United States, while it was also for the most
part rejected, where it was not ignored, in England, France and
Scandinavia. But in central Europe it became dominant, and its
exponents are found in various countries of South America and
the Far East, anthropologists who were trained in Germany,
Austria, Switzerland or Italy.

The "method" of the culture-historical school can be no
more than sketched here. Like the English diffusionists, the German group held that man is essentially an uninventive being, so
that the greater part of every culture consists of elements taken
over from elsewhere. These elements, however, were conceived
as having travelled as complexes, composed of independent items,
which by using the criteria of "form" and "quantity" could be

identified and the historical contacts between the peoples whose cultures manifested them be discerned. The more difficult relationships, involving two or more complexes, were to be disentangled by using these criteria to discover the degree to which given elements were organically a part of their cultural setting, or intrusive. In this, the factor of geographical contiguity could be ignored. Complexes that were identifiably the same in the cultures of two regions, even if the two were far distant, were held to prove that previous association must have taken place. These complexes, however, need not be made up of cultural items functionally related to one another, or having similar meanings or bearing similar sanctions, and in practice were not. The items were allocated on the basis of form alone, and each, in its own setting of use and meaning, was independent of the others—like a crutch-shaped canoe paddle and a rectangular, gable-roofed house.

Boas' critique of this "method" again throws as much light on his own positive approach as it does on the points in the Graebnerian system with which he took issue. It was published in *Science,* in 1911, as a long review of Graebner's book, written while Boas was lecturing and conducting research at the newly established International School of Archaeology and Ethnology in Mexico City which he had been instrumental in founding. Accepting Graebner's statement of the deficiencies in the classical comparative approach, he nevertheless enters a demurrer to this other attack, self-named "*the* method of ethnology," to employ Boas' italics. The point hammered home again and again in the review-article is the lack of justification for any approach to the study of culture which holds it to be something that can be understood apart from its meaning for those who live in accord with it. The exclusion from Graebner's work of any consideration of the psychological aspect of culture thus seemed to Boas "to give to the whole 'Method' a mechanical character."

For Boas, that is, to study culture and neglect the human factor was unthinkable. "It is a curious view that is so often held," he says in this same paper, "that when we speak of the influence of environment upon the human mind, only the environment need be considered. Is not in every problem of interaction the character of each of the interacting phenomena of equal importance?" The *a priori* assumption, taken as established fact by Graebner, was, also, from the point of view of basic scientific approach, unacceptable to him. "Instead of operating with the purely mechanical concept of transmission and conservation relating to the most ancient types of culture, we must investigate the innumerable cases of transmission that happen under our very eyes and try to understand how transmission is brought about and what are the conditions that favor the grouping of certain new elements of an older culture." And, as concerns the matter of regarding similarities in cultures far removed from one another as valid data for developing historical reconstructions, "I . . . repeat the warning that I have given again and again for twenty years: to be rather overcautious in admitting transmission as the cause of analogies in cases of the sporadic occurrence of similar phenomena, than to operate with the concept of lost links of a chain of cultural intercourse."

4

Boas' position as regards the study of culture, and its effect on the lives of men, cannot be labelled with a word, as evolutionism can be used to summarize the work of Tylor, or environmentalism that of Ratzel, or diffusionism that of Graebner. The range of Boas' interests, his critical scrutiny of each new hypothesis he encountered, his emphasis on method and the collection of data, the very manner in which he presented his ideas, militated against this. With his basic approach, he would, however, "be always clearly conscious of the sharp line between attractive theory and the observation that has been secured by hard and earnest work."

The massive achievement of Boas in the field of descriptive ethnography would alone be sufficient to give him an outstanding place in his science. His early work among the Eskimo, and his decades of research among the Indians of the Northwest Coast were complemented by studies among the Indians of the South-west, of the Plains area, of California. Much of his materials was presented as text and translation, yielding not only ethnographic information, but linguistic data. He carried on his researches whenever he could have recourse to those from whom he could obtain information. The Mundau, Kamba Simango, who was a student at Teacher's College, Columbia, not only provided him with materials on the social organization of his people, but with folklore and other data. Boas brought Miss Ella Deloria, a Dakota Indian, to New York so that he could work with her on a grammar of the Dakota language.

One of the explanations why Boas could collect such vast amounts of data lies in the physical strength and stamina he added to the motivating drive underlying his research. When he was almost seventy years old, he undertook a field-trip to the Pacific Northwest, taking two of his advanced graduate students with him. The only living accommodations available for the party were at a distance of several miles from where the Indians lived, with no transportation available to take them back and forth. Daily, after an early breakfast, Boas and his students would walk to the Indian encampment; daily they would return to base for lunch, and then set out again for the afternoon session. Similar tales told of Boas in Mexico, and in Porto Rico, where he went to conduct research in archaeology and physical anthropology only a few weeks after an operation on his face for the removal of a cancerous growth, reveal a consistent pattern of utter devotion to his work. A. A. Goldenweiser, indeed, recounted how, on visiting Boas in the hospital after this operation, which deprived him of the use of the muscles of the left side of his face, he found him practicing Kwakiutl phonetics with his half-paralyzed mouth!

Even more important in gathering ethnographic data was his remarkable ability to gain rapport with the Indians he studied, and his ingenuity in sensing and utilizing every possible source of data. For years, one of his old friends among the Kwakiutl wrote him periodically, in the native language, recounting the happenings in his village. Not only did these data document the ways in which the broad patterns of the culture were manifest in actual behavior, but they also revealed much concerning the personal relations between members of the village, and how these individuals adjusted to one another in meeting the exigencies of daily life. It is unfortunate that Boas never found the opportunity to publish these letters, as he intended. They kept him abreast of the affairs of the people, giving him the knowledge that enabled him, in the moving experiences of the last years of his life, when he made his final visit to them, to sit with the old men he had known so long and discuss with them, as an elder among the elders of the tribe, the things in which they were all interested, as though he had never been away.

This ability to attain rapport stemmed from the recognition he accorded values in the life of the peoples with whom he dealt, the deep pity he felt for the difficult times on which they had come, and his honest humility in the face of those who commanded information whose importance he understood, and which he had come to them to learn. In his own culture, Boas, though a man of broad human sympathy, was proud, with a sense of position that derived from the early days of his childhood training. He would concede what he felt to be his due to no man; but where he was the student, he took the position that those who taught him merited the respect that he gave them. It is as though the hardships of his year among the Eskimo had read him a lesson he never forgot, impounded in the depths of his unconscious thinking; for the kind of rapport he could obtain is not easily achieved with peoples who have been the victims of historic forces such as have played on the American Indians. It cannot be had at all, indeed, except where honesty of purpose in the student is so basic, and understanding so complete, that is is evidenced in attitude and behavior and does not have to be expressed in words. Only then will those who are among the deprived peoples of the earth reveal the things they hold important, and even sacred, to a member of the race which has taken from them the right to live in accordance with their traditional ways and, as bitter experience has taught, in doing this has depreciated and caused to be despised their most precious values.

The data which Boas, directly or indirectly, caused to be collected by his students and his associates cannot be ignored in evaluating his contribution to the study of culture. The four decades of the tenure of his professorship at Columbia gave a continuity to his teaching that permitted him to develop students who eventually made up the greater part of the significant professional core of American anthropologists, and who came to man and direct most of the major departments of anthropology in the United States. In their turn, they have trained the students who, with the increase in general interest in the subject and the recognition of the contribution it can make to human knowledge and human welfare, have continued in the tradition in which their teachers were trained, especially the tradition of basing theory on empirical data, and of employing first-hand study in the field to obtain these data.

It should not be assumed, of course, that Boas originated the practice of doing field research, or that he initiated its techniques. In the United States, Morgan, Powell, Mooney, Bandelier and other precursors lived with the Indians, and organized their observations into accounts that continue to stand as important contributions to ethnological science. But they differed from Boas in several respects. For one thing, few of them were professionals in the sense that he was—Morgan was a lawyer, Mooney an army officer, Powell a geologist. Those who held university teaching posts occupied their chairs for too short a period to permit the impact of their work to be felt in the future development of their science through the accomplishments of a corps of students trained by them. Again, unlike Boas, the field reports they produced, when these were not by-products of other assignments, or studies made during time snatched from other pursuits, were not ordinarily designed to analyze a particular problem.

In Europe, too, the tradition of field work had been growing, but here a more subtle factor entered. The peoples studied by European anthropologists lived at great distances from the home base. Most often, too, research was carried on in the colonial possessions of the country to which the anthropologist belonged. A case can be made for the equation which treats the American Indian as the counterpart of the native inhabitant of the colony of a European power, but in fact the difference in traditional approach of members of the dominant group toward the two was so great as to make this unrealistic. The Indian, whatever the attitude toward him may have been on the frontier, was thought of as an integral part of the American scene. Not only this, but the absence of a system of native administration comparable to that in the colonies of the Far East, Africa, and the South Seas made it the exception, rather than the rule, for the anthropologist, studying an Indian group, to identify himself with the reservation superintendent rather than with the Indians.

Whatever the case, it was the rule for Boas and his students to live among the peoples they studied whenever circumstances permitted, or as close to them as possible where such arrangements could not be made. In the earlier days of field research, they were engaged essentially in recovering the memories of a past no longer lived by the Indians, so that far more time was given to taking down accounts of earlier ways from the elders than in observing the changes going on about them. Yet the work was done man to man, in the setting of the community under study. One need but read the sketches by Boas and others who contributed to the volume of stories edited by Elsie Clews Parsons under the title *American Indan Life* to realize the degree to which they lived the life they described, and were conscious of its human no less than its institutional manifestations.

This perhaps is why Boas found it difficult to understand how the doctrine of functionalism, developed by B. Malinowski on the basis of his field research in the Trobriand Islands, and given its name about 1925, constituted a major contribution to anthropological science. The impact of Malinowski's work on English anthropology lay in the insistence in his writing that it come out of the study into the field; but in the United States it was, and had from the beginning been in the field and, with a few exceptions, had never been confined to the study. Malinowski's contribution to research on the economics of nonliterate peoples did not apparently have any appreciable interest for Boas, since he never referred to it, though this may have been because the economic aspects of the cultures he himself studied never formed a focus of his concern.

One of his few published comments on Malinowski's work is buried in a review, written in 1926, of Malinowski's *Crime and Custom in Savage Society*. Its "principal merit," he states, "lies in the close observation and description of the daily life of a primitive people." Yet, despite the value of its materials Boas finds that "some of the theoretical conclusions" are "not . . . so well founded." To derive dual divisions in society from the give and take of reciprocal obligations seems unjustified, since "obligations cross one another in a great variety of ways." Moreover, "Dr. Malinowski has a strange impression of what modern anthropology is. He accuses modern anthropologists of a complete disregard of the actualities of life and of a restriction in their endeavors to see only the standardized forms of life which are considered as absolutely rigid and binding." On the contrary, Boas asserts, Malinowski "will find that the general approach of the modern American anthropologists is quite similar to his own."

What caused Boas to reject Malinowski's position in general was not that his study of a culture was descriptive and analytical, with a strong psychological bent, for this was Boas' approach, but that it was ahistorical if not anti-historical. "An attempt to explain the details of the behavior of a people on purely psychological grounds can never give an adequate understanding of the cultural life as it exists today. . . . The very complexity of historical development . . . contradicts the assumption that supposedly existing 'laws' of psychology, no matter how much we may value the study of social behavior, can ever replace the necessity of an historical approach to ethnic phenomena." For Boas, to neglect the historical component, since it involved cutting oneself off from an obvious facet of human experience, seemed so preposterous that he no more gave time to the ahistorical theory of functionalism than to the caricature of historical method advanced by Elliot Smith. And it is worth noting that though Malinowski attacked him, sometimes bitterly, he never replied to these attacks.

Functionalism, as an approach to field data, and thus as a tool and not a theory, was in essence nothing new to Boas, who had written in 1895: "The incorporation (of borrowed elements) into the mythology of the tribe is due to the peculiar social organization which favors the introduction of any myth . . . if it promises to enhance the social positon of the clan." In his later research, he traced the reflection of Tsimshian life in Tsimshian mythology, or demonstrated the role that the carved totem-pole of the Kwakiutl played in their social organiztaion, or, as has been mentioned, showed how Vandau kinship terminology was an essential factor in maintaining the social sanctions that this people live by.

In short, just as Boas accepted the possibility of regular sequences of events without being an "evolutionist," and the principle of diffusion without becoming a "diffusionist," he recognized the fact of the integration of culture and that it functioned to fill needs in human life without being a "functionalist." In his reaction to all these approaches, we see, time and again, how in the selectivity of his point of view, the need for ground-clearing operations was so patent to him that he was content when his eclecticism prevailed over what he regarded as their excesses.

The controversy that so continuously characterized his treatment of ethnological theory has been the cause of much misunderstanding of his contribution. In an analysis of his approach to linguistics, published in 1944 in the first issue of the resuscitated *International Journal of American Linguistics*, which Boas founded in 1917, Roman Jakobson well makes the point: "He often presented his discoveries as a mere criticism of current theories. . . . He fervently insisted on 'limitations of comparative method,' but he did not strive to make clear that in fact his outlook upon diffusion is destined first of all for enlarging the limits of historical comparison. . . ." Or, as he summarizes it, "News on the discovery of America would be given by Boas as a disproof of the hypothesis on the shorter way to India, while data on the new part of the world would be mentioned only casually."

If no label can be applied to Boas, however, this is undoubtedly as he would have had it. The need of his time was the development of theory in terms of data whose validity could stand the test of scientific analysis, and this meant testing all approaches. The methods whereby such data are to be obtained were largely his work; and the theoretical basis of his science is the more secure because of the critiques he lodged against the positions he deemed untenable.

5

The magnitude of the positive contribution Boas made to the understanding of culture is to be grasped through the realization that the two currents which flow most strongly in mid-Twentieth Century anthropology, and constitute primary contributions to an understanding of human socal life, have their historical sources in his work. One of these is to be subsumed under the heading of cultural dynamics, the second of the psychology of culture.

In 1896, Boas wrote the following passage: "It will be well to restate at this place one of the principal aims of anthropological research. We agreed that certain laws exist which govern the growth of human culture, and it is our endeavor to discover these laws. The object of our investigation is to find the *processes* by which certain stages of culture have developed. The customs and beliefs themselves are not the ultimate objects of research. We desire to learn the reasons why such customs and beliefs exist. . . ." In 1920, he phrased the problem in these terms: "The activities of the individual are determined to a great extent by his social environment, but in turn his own activities influence the society in which he lives, and may bring about modifications in its form. Obviously, this problem is one of the most important ones to be taken up in a study of cultural changes. It is also beginning to attract the attention of students who are no longer satisfied with the systematic enumeration of standardized beliefs and customs of a tribe, but who begin to be interested in the question of the way in which the individual reacts to his whole social environment, and to the differences of opinion and of modes of action that occur in primitive society and which are the causes of far-reaching changes."

This, however, was anything but simple where the actual

processes of change could not be observed, and historical relationships could only be reconstructed. This is why, by the logic of its problem, anthropology came to study cultural change in process or, as it is called, acculturation—a word, it may be said, Boas, following Powell and Homes, used in its modern sense as long ago as 1896 in his paper, "The Growth of Indian Mythologies." He actually did carry on some research in the problem of the effect of contact between peoples, as is seen in his discussion, published in 1925, of the influence of Romance folk-lore on the tales of American Indians. But, in the main, it remained for those who came after him to develop the techniques of studying cultural dynamics through research among peoples, both literate and without written languages, actually undergoing change in their cultures through contact with other modes of life.

The psychological approach to culture was fundamental in Boas' thinking. From the first, he insisted that it be taken into full account, and often referred to cultural, as against physical, anthropology as the "mental" side of the sicence. He numbered such psychologists among his students as E. L. Thorndike and R. H. Woodworth, while his association with Cattell made for mutual influencing of concept and approach. To him it was clear that man was no automaton, carried through the ages on the back of his cultures, but that culture was a product of human mentality, influencing human behavior deeply, reciprocally influenced by the reaction of individuals to it. At Boas' death, one of the obituary notices in *Science* was entitled "Franz Boas, Psychologist." Its writer, J. P. Foley, observing that "his chief interest seems to have shifted from the anthropological description and intercomparison of cultures *per se* to the psychological description of the specific stimulating conditions under which the individual's responses are acquired," comments that "experimental social psychology has lost one of its ablest students in his death."

The psychology he espoused was that of his middle years. He was interested in the problem of the influence of culture on perception, such as was studied in Woodworth's test of differences in the perception of color and form, carried out on the representatives of nonliterate peoples exhibited at the St. Louis World's Fair in 1904. He sponsored the study by Efron of varied modes and amount of gesturing that accompanies speech among persons of different races and classes, demonstrating the influence of cultural tradition and status on this form of motor behavior.

Broader uses of psychological concepts, such as those which attempted to assign entire societies to particular categories of mental set, as in the book *Patterns of Culture* by his student and colleague Ruth Benedict, seemed to him to raise methodological questions that had not been faced. Though for personal reasons he consented to write a brief preface for the work, he devoted several paragraphs to a critical discussion of the problem in his chapter on methods of research in the textbook he edited,* especially pointed because he takes as his example the Northwest Coast Indians, who had been cited as an extreme case by Benedict. Indicating that "the leading motive of their life is the limitless pursuit of gaining social prestige and of holding on to what has been gained, and the intense feeling of inferiority and shame if even a part of the prestige is lost," he adds, "these tendencies are so striking that the amiable qualities that appear in intimate family life are easily overlooked." Certainly the almost paranoid nature of the behavior of this people as portrayed by Benedict is scarcely in line with the patterns of humility Boas sketches as prevailing within the family. He summarizes his own position with characteristic scientific realism and methodological caution: "The less pronounced the leading ideas of a simple culture, or the more varying the ideas of a tribe divided into social strata, the more difficult it is to draw a valid picture that does not contain contradictions. We cannot hope to do more than to elucidate the leading ideas, remembering clearly the limitations of their validity."

None of the approaches to human mentality that derive from the study of psychopathology ever appealed to Boas. He found the writings of Freud uncongenial, and especially rejected the symbolism that was so integral a part of the Freudian system, since what were here put forth as universals he recognized to be culture-bound; a point, indeed, that later came to be accepted even by some psychoanalysts. In one of his last papers, though

* Boas apparently regarded the matter of sufficient importance to devote a separate article to discussing it, since he used the same data to make the same point in the article "Die Individualität primitiver Kulturen" he prepared for the volume in honor of Ferdinand Tönnies, published in 1936.

"with some hesitation," he explained his position regarding "the psychiatric approach to anthropological data" in these terms: "I can see that the expression of organic mental disturbances in different cultures will lead to different manifestations and that in this sense the study of abnormal behavior may be helpful to the student of mental diseases, but I think it is very unlikely that it will help us much in understanding the normal phenomena of culture. I believe particularly that the use of psychoanalysis for attacking the problems of primitive culture can not bear the light of careful critical examination. I accept as an important contribution the effect of experiences in early life upon the personality of the indivdual, but when the attempt is made to explain mythology, totemism, taboo on the basis of psychoanalytic theories, I cannot follow. There are so many hypotheses involved in each step that it seems to me that the results can no longer be called scientifically sound." Yet even in this area, his scientific curiosity did not permit him to be satisfied with mere negation. It is not without interest to note the friendliness he manifested toward Bruno Klopfer, one of the early exponents in the United States of the use of the Rorschach test, and his interest in the application of this test to the study of cultural and racial differences in personality structure.

The development in anthropology since the end of the Second World War of the study of cultural dynamics, especially acculturation, and of the study of the relation between the individual and the culture of the society to which he belongs, have had repercussions far beyond any that might have been predicted during Boas' lifetime. The rapid post-war growth of anthropology, the contribution the concept of culture has come to make in the social sciences and the humanities, and the use of anthropological techniques as aids to achieve comprehension of foreign cultures and world cultural adjustment, are but some of the aspects of this development. Their lineage draws from various sources. But none has had greater effect than Boas' major theoretical contribution, the concept of culture as a dynamic, changing force, to be understood only if it is recognized as a manifestation of the "mental life" of man.

CHAPTER FOUR

MAN, THE CREATOR

EVERY man lives as a member of a society, ordering his behavior and shaping his thought in accordance with its patterns; yet except in the rarest instances, this is not the whole story. At some time in his life, however brief the moment, in some mode of conduct, however slight its import, he asserts his individuality. In doing so, he extends the limits that had previously bounded the forms of thought and action sanctioned by his group, and to the extent his innovation proves acceptable, becomes a force making for change in its way of life.

Where the idea or the deed is of small consequence, particularly where it deviates but slightly from accepted forms, the creative act is of little significance, except perhaps for some student seeking to understand the modes and mechanisms of change. But the new ideas and unconventional deeds of some men and women may cause reorientations which bring on changes in those fundamental beliefs and values that are charged with emotion and, when questioned, challenge the faithful to defend the established way. Then a time of tension, uncertainty and strife may set in, to endure until social equilibrium is once more established, and what was thought of as daring innovation becomes accepted convention.

That change is a universal in the history of every human society, initiated by the individual, who moves within the limits of his culture even when it seems to him that he is most strongly revolting against it, is a proposition which was by no means always accepted. Earlier students of culture, especially in think-ing of "primitive" man, conceived him as living in a kind of cultural strait-jacket, manifesting a degree of conservatism un-known in what they regarded as the higher civilizations of Europe and America.

This point of view was in some measure due to the fact that the societies described in these terms were without writing. These peoples thus could tell no tale of the alteration of custom over the generations, as could those whose written records permitted differences between past and present conventions to be analyzed. Even more important, however, was the fact that the traditions of the so-called "simpler" societies, seen without the perspective of time-depth, seemed rigid, fixed and unchanging because they were observed by outsiders, who had neither the time, the oppor-tunity, the training nor the interest to grasp the variations in behavior that were the expression of differences which testified to the creativity of the individual in these cultures.

Such writers as Herbert Spencer, Sir Henry Maine, or later, Lester Ward, who were prominent among those responsible for establishing this picture of utter conservatism, were what has come to be termed "arm-chair anthropologists." Employing what others had written of these "primitives," they saw their subjects through the eyes of men whose vision, befogged by haste, or conviction, or special interest, perceived a consensus of conduct among the peoples observed by them, not the differences between the behavior of one individual and another out of which such a consensus rises. The generalized portrayal of behavior thus pre-sented not only strengthened the concept of conservatism, but fed back through this concept to observers who came to look only for the consensus, and dismissed variations as of no consequence. It took many years of patient study to ferret out the nature of this illusion, and to correct the false perspective it engendered.

Perhaps it was because Boas, from his early expedition to the Eskimo, had first-hand contact with the peoples he studied, that we never find this point of view in his writings. He agreed, on the whole, that "primitive" people are more prone to be con-servative than are larger literate groupings. But, accepting the postulate of the unity of man, he ascribed this to such factors as their smallness of number, or their relative isolation; nor did he maintain that their cultures could not change, or would not, when the stimulus of contact with other peoples, or of innovations arising within the group, was experienced. For him, a "primitive" man was never a lay figure, an automaton responding blindly to the preestablished customs of his society, not able to change the conventions handed down to him from his forebears even if he wished to do so. He knew better; the Eskimo and the Indians with whom he had lived were men like himself—inventive, able to think through their problems, and by no means without critical insights into their own ways.

How early in his career the role of the individual in society came to be of importance to him is to be seen from a lecture he delivered in 1888 before a German society in New York, concerned with the problems of science. This contribution, included in translation under the title, "The Aims of Ethnology," in his volume of collected papers, shows insights that are the more remarkable precisely because thinking on the subject at that time was so different. "It is instructive to see how difficult it is to adopt new ideas," he says. "The invention is not difficult. Difficult is the retention and further development. Therefore . . . it is important to observe the fight of individuals against tribal customs. The same kind of struggle the genius has to undergo among ourselves in his battle against dominant ideas or dominant prejudice occurs among primitives and it is of particular interest to see in how far the strong individual is able to free himself from the fetters of convention."

A decade and a half later, in a short paper entitled "The Ethnological Significance of Esoteric Doctrines," Boas called for a reappraisal of the emphasis being placed by anthropologists on the study of the secret knowledge of Indian tribes, lodged in the hands of the elders, to the neglect of the broader base of belief found among the ordinary members, not privy to the "symbolic significance of complex rites, and the philosophic views of nature they reveal." Contrary to the prevailing point of view, he maintained that "the esoteric doctrine must, to a great extent, be considered as the product of individual thought," which shows "a mutual and probably inextricable interrelation" between it and the body of exoteric, or popular beliefs.

For Boas, the esoteric knowledge of a tribe was to be thought of as "the reaction of the best minds in the community to the general cultural environment." Because of this, such doctrines "must be treated like any other system of philosophy, and its study has the same aims as the study of the history of philosophy." Yet while they were to be collected, analyzed and understood by anthropologists. more widely spread ideas must not be neglected. "It has taken many years," he observes at the end of this paper, "for the study of the culture of civilized people to broaden out so as to take in not only the activities of the great, but also the homely life of the masses. . . . If it is true that for a full understanding of civilized society the knowledge of the popular mind is a necessity, it is doubly true in more primitive forms of society, where the isolation of social groups is very slight, and where each and every individual is connected by a thousand ties with the majority of the members of the tribe to which he belongs." The official point of view, so to speak, must of course be recorded. "Only let us not lose sight of their intimate relation to the popular beliefs, of the necessity of studying the two in connection with each other, and of the error we should commit if we should consider the esoteric doctrine, and the whole system of thought and of ethical ideals which it represents, as the only true form of the inner life of the Indian."

The concept of the importance of the individual in influencing social behavior has flowered in more specific research, on a cross-cultural basis, through the collection of life-histories, through intensive investigation into the different ways in which, in a given society, the same end may be attained, through the tradition of recording opinions that show disagreement from accepted custom as well as describing custom in its prevailing form. Out of these analyses have come the concepts of "real" and "ideal" culture, a concise phrasing of the fact that individuals everywhere do not necessarily practice what they preach; and that, as concerns some individuals, what they actually practice goes beyond what anyone in their society preaches.

The interest Boas showed in the individual, which grew out of his concern with cultural dynamics, led him to insist that the study of the aspects of culture where individual creativity is most manifest be accorded a full place in the repertory of anthropological interest. In essence, this meant that he included in all his research humanistic phases of the cultures of the peoples he studied as well as their social institutions. This is the more striking because Boas' orientation, both by training and temperament, was essentially that of the scientist. His mathematical bent was fundamental; he phrased his approach to problems in the conventional terms of hypotheses to be tested by reference to the data; he mistrusted intuitions and excoriated any position that had what he considered to be a component of mysticism. He liked music, and playing the piano gave him great pleasure and afforded a means of relaxation; but his taste in music was highly conventional, as were the rigid criteria he applied to literature and the graphic and plastic arts.

What is important is that, as between the study of the social life of man and its humanistic, creative aspects, he held a balance that has been all too rare in the study of man. If he refrained from defining his area of study as the social institutions of man, as many anthropologists have done, he did not, in analogous manner, restrict it to these other phases. All the activities of a people he studied came under his purview, or as many as he could effectively study. Where he wrote on one of them, he related them to life as a whole, making his presentation a matter of emphasis rather than exclusiveness. Hence we have the apparent paradox of this scientist according the study of the humanistic phases of culture the same attention as the institutional; giving to those creative aspects, that derive from the sensibilities and intuitions which he distrusted when confronted with them in his own culture, an importance equal to that he gave the social structures which, on the surface, can be studied in terms of obvious regularities.

In truth, Boas, the scientist, was a great humanist. He pointed the way toward the use of cross-cultural studies as a bridge to bring together the social sciences and the humanistic disciplines, an approach that is coming to be recognized as an indispensable prerequisite to a unified science of man. Because he was in essence a humanist, his contributions in the fields of linguistics, folklore and the graphic and plastic arts hold a major position in his theoretical and methodological approach to culture. And though he never wrote on philosophy as such, his writings afford a significant point of departure for the reorientation philosophy must undergo if the role of culture in shaping perception and thought is adequately to be taken into account in seeking to understand the many differing ideas man has developed to explain himself and the universe in which he lives.

2

Boas was a self-made linguist. Yet, as Roman Jakobson has pointed out in his perceptive evaluation of Boas' contribution to this field from which we have already quoted, though "he came from natural sciences with a demand for reliable and rigid methods . . . he had no ambitions to force naturalistic habits on the humanities." Rather he was able to see fresh opportunities in the study of language, opportunities to which he brought his critical insights, while "he remained free of the various prejudices and antiquated survivals which weighed heavily on linguistics and ethnology."

As in all his anthropological achievement, the importance of the fact that his contacts with the people he studied were at first-hand cannot be overestimated. In proper context, language became an integral part of the culture, and its unaccustomed categories fell into place when used in the setting for which they were intended. As he put it, ". . . from practical, as well as from theoretical points of view, the study of language must be considered as one of the most important branches of ethnological study, because, on the one hand, a thorough insight into ethnology cannot be gained without practical knowledge of language, and, on the other hand, the fundamental concepts illustrated by human languages are not distinct in kind from ethnological phenomena; and because, furthermore, the peculiar characteristics of languages are clearly reflected in the views and customs of the peoples of the world."

With his early recognition of the importance of language as

an integral part of the study of culture, Boas came also to understand the need to discover the range of variation in the structure and functioning of this precise, intricate instrument. New approaches were here necessary. He early realized that the Indo-European languages represented but one possible group of forms, and comprised but one historic stream among the tongues of mankind and the linguistic families of the world. From this, he moved to the analysis of the sounds of speech, of the way in which these sounds are fashioned into the units that make up the vocabulary of a people, and of the morphology of language as shown in its grammatical structure. But he went beyond this, from form to meaning which, in turn, brought him the full round to the importance of language, as an aspect of culture, for the student who would assess to the full the way of life he was studying.

It is essential here, as in other facets of his work, to set Boas' contribution to the field of linguistics in the perspective of its time to grasp its measure of worth. Most of those whose lives led them to the far places of the earth for more than casual visits recognized the importance of achieving at least rudimentary communication with the people with whom they had to deal. Those who were linguistically gifted, or felt the need of making the language available to others, applied themselves to writing grammars and dictionaries of the unwritten languages they had learned. Many were missionaries, who translated the Bible for the benefit of those to whom they ministered. But one need only glance at the works they wrote, valuable as they remain to give time-depth to the research of later students, to perceive that their dictionaries and grammars followed the model of those to which they were accustomed, and that they transcribed the words and phrases they set down in terms of sounds they had assimilated to their own phonetic patterns.

Boas was among the first to insist that the sounds of Indo-European and Semitic languages and their grammatical categories represented but two possible means of linguistic expression; that each new tongue studied must therefore be analyzed in terms of its own forms, however bizarre these might seem to the outsider. Thus in 1906, in addressing a plea to the American Philological Association to take up American Indian research, he said, "The psychological foundation and morphological development of American languages are so peculiar that their study must be a revelation to the student of Indo-European or of Semitic languages. Well-known problems which you have discussed for years appear in new aspects, and broad points of view for discussion of linguistic questions present themselves readily to the student who takes up the types of language peculiar to our continent."

This principle, revolutionary in its day, has given rise to the discipline of comparative linguistics, and has continuously illuminated the systematic study of the vast number of unwritten languages spoken over the world. It has become so basic in the study of language in general, indeed, that it is no longer a matter for discussion. No more do we find grammars and dictionaries of unwritten languages, compiled by those who would call themselves linguists, that take for their models those of French or German or English or Spanish. In the light of the principle that languages must be studied inductively, in terms of their own orientations, such attempts take on a kind of quaintness that demonstrates how far from its earlier ethnocentrisms linguistic science has moved. It is difficult to realize how recently Boas and his students opened the door to this approach by accepting as valid what seemed the most unlikely modes of expression, and developed a tradition of investigation whereby the unusual, in terms of earlier assumptions concerning the nature of linguistic forms and linguistic structure, could be understood as normal in its own cultural setting.

The project which culminated in the monumental *Handbook of American Languages* afforded Boas an opportunity to present his position with full documentation, consisting of the grammars of hitherto unanalyzed Indian tongues, three of them written by Boas himself, each set forth in accordance with its own phonetic principles and its own grammatical rules. His position concerning the nature of language, and how and why it should be studied, is set forth in the 80-page "Introduction," a classic document that has influenced ethnology no less than linguistics, because here, as always, he related the study of language to the study of culture, enriching both in the process.

Characteristically, it begins with a consideration of the problems that have arisen out of attempts "to determine the position of the American race" by reference to physical type, or language, or culture. Boas here demonstrates that these three, for purposes of drawing classifications, are independent variables, in that categories based on any one of them will not hold for the others. This leads to the important methodological principle that the end of research, where these factors are concerned, is not to determine the position of a people in a "more or less artificial" system of classifying mankind, but to establish the lines of historical development in a given instance.

What follows is, in effect, an early text-book in what would later come to be termed the field of comparative linguistics. The years that have passed since these pages were written have brought much in the way of greater precision of terminology, refinement of method, and shift in emphasis. The directions they pointed, however, still guide those who are concerned either with the study of languages or the understanding of the nature of language—two quite different things, both of which are by no means always taken into account in the work of linguists. It is all there, however—the structural approach, the historical and classificatory point of view, and the psychology of language and its relation to the way of life of a people, or what some have termed "ethnolinguistics," and others, who emphasize meaning, call semantics.

Through the entire essay, one finds the basic theme of Boas' approach to all facets of learned behavior—the historical derivation of what seems at first glance an arbitrary selection of a given form out of a vast range of possibility, and the seeming inevitability of the trait, once selected, to the people who have incorporated it in their culture. Thus, at the outset, after a conventional definition of the nature of speech, we read that while "the number of sounds that may be produced in this manner is unlimited," yet ". . . every single language has a definite and limited group of sounds, and that the number of those used in any particular dialect is never excessively large."

This consistency, though granted for Indo-European tongues, was not recognized in others. Boas thus moved to enquire why accuracy of pronunciation was not believed to be as evident,

or of as much significance, in "primitive" American Indian languages as it was "in the languages of the civilized world." His
answer is not found in the languages studied, but in their students:
"It would seem that this view is based largely on the fact that
certain sounds . . . are interpreted by observers sometimes as
one European sound, sometimes another." The psychological insight in this observation is as valid as the methodological principle
it implies has been found to be. We have come to recognize that
the effective sound-units, the phonemes, of a language are standardized versions about which play the linguistically insignificant
variations of the speakers. Some of these sounds, however, distinct
though they may be for those who use a given language, when
heard by a non-speaker, are assimilated to his previous speech
conditioning. Thus the sound in Pawnee, "an exceedingly weak *r*"
is heard by English speakers at times as *l*, at others as *r, n* or *d*.
Conversely, Northwest Coast Indians hear the *cl* in the English
word *close* sometimes as *tl*, sometimes as *cl*, sometimes as *gl*. As
Boas put it, "the alternation of the sounds is clearly an effect of
perception through the medium of a foreign system of phonetics,
not that of a greater variability of pronunciation than the one that
is characteristic of our own sounds."

The same principle of arbitrary selection is found in grammar. "Since the total range of personal experience which language
serves to express is infinitely varied, and its whole scope must be
expressed by a limited number of phonetic groups, it is obvious
that an extended classification of experiences must underlie all
articulate speech." Here again we come on the standardization of
variants permitted within limits, so that within a given group, an
individual can communicate to his fellows his own perceptions
or emotional responses, which are never identical to those of the
one to whom he speaks. But just as the individual variations within a group are so slight as to be functionally insignificant, the
possibilities of expressing the same idea in different ways seem
endless.

We may choose at random one instance which Boas cites to
make this point. "Logically," he says, "our three persons of the
pronoun are based on the two concepts of self and not-self, the
second of which is subdivided, according to the needs of speech

into the two concepts of person addressed and person spoken of."
Yet, though this seems self-evident to us, the Sioux make no dis-
tinction in pronouns between second person singular and plural,
and only an imperfect differentiation in the third person where
number is concerned. All emphasis, that is, seems here to be laid
on distinguishing singular or plural in the first person. Or, to take
another instance, though in English the word *this* is adequate as a
demonstrative to imply any singular object reasonably near the
speaker, the Eskimo must specify the direction in which it lies
from the one using it. The term *this man* would thus become:

> *This man near me*
> *near thee*
> *near him*
> *in front of me*
> *behind me*
> *to the right of me*
> *to the left of me*
> *above me*
> *below me, etc.*

In the case of the Kwakiutl, it is essential to indicate whether the
object to which reference is had can be seen by the speaker or
not: *this (singular or plural) house visible near me,* or . . . *in-
visible near me,* and the like.

We may pass over Boas' discussion of the problem of historical relationships between Indian languages and the bearing
of this on the task of drawing classifications of these unwritten
tongues. His position here was essentially the one he assumed in
the study of any aspect of culture. Historic connection can be
safely assumed only between modes of speech "for which we can
give proof of relationship that cannot possibly be challenged."
The fact of diffusion, and the absence of written records that
enable students of Indo-European languages to document their
assumptions of historic borrowing, made him wary of the so-
called "language-families" that had been suggested, for example,
by Major Powell in an undertaking to which Boas makes no
reference in this paper. This position he continued to maintain.
In 1920 and later in 1929, he published papers bearing the

identical title "The Classification of American Indian Languages." His conclusion is stated at the end of the later one, ". . . it is not possible to group American languages rigidly in a genealogical scheme in which each linguistic family is shown to have developed to modern forms, but we have to recognize that many of the languages have multiple roots." His point of view, however, was not in the prevailing current. It brought him into controversy with such an outstanding linguist, his own student, as Edward Sapir, among others of those he had trained; and developments since his death have carried further the approach of which he disapproved. But, as always, he held fast to what seemed to him to be methodologically sound, and included both his 1920 and 1929 statements in the volume of collected papers he published a decade later.

One of Boas' remarkable insights into the nature of linguistic phenomena is found in his discussion, in the "Introduction" to the *Handbook*, of the theoretical importance of linguistics, where he points out the unconscious ease with which speakers of a particular language manipulate their patterns of speech. This arose out of his conviction that, "as a part of ethnological phenomena in general," language must be thought of as another manifestation of the "mental" life of man. As he phrased it, "the use of language is so automatic that the opportunity never arises for the fundamental notions to emerge into consciousness."

Language thus lies at the extreme end of the continuum of consciousness of various aspects of culture, whereby "the linguistic classifications never rise into consciousness, while in other ethnological phenomena, although the same unconscious origin prevails, these often rise into consciousness, and thus give rise to secondary reasoning and to reinterpretations." From this the conclusion is reached, that "the great advantage that linguistics offer in this respect is the fact that, on the whole, the categories which are formed always remain unconscious, and that for this reason the processes which lead to their formation can be followed without the misleading and disturbing factors of secondary explanations, which are so common in ethnology, so much so that they generally obscure the real history of the development of ideas generally."

Boas was deeply interested in the influence of language on thought, as is seen in the discussion of the problem in this early memoir. But though his writing foreshadows the position that later developed into what has become known as semantics, he never ascribed to speech the power to control thought. He used the phrase "semantic significance," and underscored the proposition that without grasping the essential meaning of the words used by a people, a full understanding of their thinking could not be attained. Yet despite this, Sapir's dictum that "language is an index to culture," though it would seem to fit Boas' positon, went farther than he was willing to go.

Especially as concerns vocabulary, he continually referred to instances that showed how differently different societies can categorize experience. The illustration he most favored, perhaps, and one that was made familiar to the many students who sat under him or under those trained by him or to those who encountered it in his published works, had to do with the varied Eskimo ways of expressing the concept for which the single verbal symbol "snow" suffices the speaker of English. "Here," he wrote, "we find one word expressing 'snow on the ground'; another one 'falling snow'; a third one 'drifting snow'; a fourth one 'a snow-drift.' " Or, from the same language, he drew the further instance of the word "seal," which, though for English speakers is a self-sufficient linguistic generalization and one which the Eskimo also have, is for them supplemented by other terms for "seal basking in the sun," "seal floating on a piece of ice," in addition to "the many names for the seals of different ages and for male and female."

Obviously, these semantic orientations reflect the interests of the peoples who use them, as Boas freely admitted. But the case of grammatical categories was more difficult. "There is little doubt but thought is thus directed in various channels," he stated in a paper entitled "Language and Culture" written for a volume honoring Waldo G. Leland on his retirement as director of the American Council of Learned Societies, and published only a few months before Boas died. "If I say 'the father built a new house for his son,' and the Indian says 'the son was the reason for his father's housebuilding,' we stress purpose, the Indian causality. Such a tendency pervading the language may well lead to a different reaction to the incidents of everyday life and it is conceivable that in this sense the mental activities of a people may be in part directed by language. I should not be inclined the overestimate this influence, because devices for expressing finality as over against causality are ever-present, and may rise into idiomatic use." A concise statement summarizes his position in the matter: "I think our general experience in the field of linguistic data proves that language is a reflex of culture and that there are everywhere linguistic devices that enable the language to follow the demands of culture."

What he would never concede, and where time has richly vindicated him, was that any language may be regarded as superior to another or, as has been so often claimed, that greater propensity to generalize indicates a higher stage of development, either linguistic or cultural. Even where linguistic abstrations are not a part of the current vocabulary of a people, Boas demonstrated out of his own field work that they could be conceptualized. As in the case of race, so of speech; there is no inferior language. In this same paper, asserting that "the obligatory categories of language differ fundamentally," he pointed out that the "rigid localization" of some Indian languages has advantages that might be worth copying by ourselves. "It will be obvious that the mental picture aroused by a spoken sentence will be fundamentally different accordng to these categories. We could read our newspapers with much greater satisfaction if our language would compel them to say whether their reports are based on self-experience, inference, or hearsay!"

3

Boas' interest in the oral arts and their accompanying forms— tale and myth, poetry, music and dance—was closely linked to his concern with linguistics. He early recognized that to understand the cultural behavior of a people one must grasp their underlying system of implicit assumptions and explicit standards, and that to achieve this a knowledge of the language is essential. One of the ways in which linguistic materials could best be collected was through writing down texts, dictated by a speaker of the unwritten language being studied. Long before the day of electronic recording equipment, even before phonographs were available for field research, it was obvious that the best linguistic data lay in the myths and tales of the Indians, which, taken in the original tongue, would yield "objective material which will stand the scrutiny of painstaking investigation," as Boas put it. There is no more characteristic aspect of his work, and that of his students, than is to be found in the many volumes of text and translations they edited; materials that document the literary artistry of the peoples from whom the collections were obtained, as well as their ethnographic and linguistic patterns.

Boas was never the nooks-and-cranny type of folklorist. The exotic, the quaint, in the lives of those held not to have reached the level of cultural sophistication ascribed to Europe and America, had little meaning for him. In this, his approach was in the full current of American thought, his position being quite in accord with that of the other anthropologists·and students of the humanities he joined in founding the American Folklore Society. "Survivals" of full-blown customs of earlier times, like those found in the peasant cultures of Europe, were simply not present in American society. On the frontier, whether among Indians or explorers or settlers, the folklore to be studied was contained in the literary expressions of the people. Custom, where Indian ways were concerned, was obviously to be treated as ethnography; in the case of white Americans, as economics or sociology or history.

The collections of the literary forms of aboriginal peoples of North America made by Boas are as impressive as the store of data he gathered in other fields of anthropology. If to his own materials be added the contributions of his students, and of those whom he influenced to record collections of stories in text and translation, we almost encompass the field to the time of his death. He not only edited the *Journal of American Folk-Lore* from 1908 until 1923, filling its pages with primary materials, but also the substantial volumes of *Memoirs* that were likewise published by the Society. In addition, the early volumes of the *Columbia University Contributions to Anthropology*, which also appeared under his editorship, are filled with texts, mainly of myths and tales, in native languages, with their translations. But Boas caused more than just Indian materials to be collected and published. From time to time, an entire number of the *Journal* would be devoted to folk-tales from French Canada; he encouraged the extensive work of Elsie Clews Parsons in collecting Negro folk-tales; he was instrumental in sending Manuel Andrade to the Dominican Republic to gather materials on Spanish folklore in the Caribbean.

Boas was as always more than the collector; though here, as in other aspects of his work, his theoretical concerns were likely to be lost in the mass of his documentation, and the almost casual manner in which he presented them, either as comments on a given body of data or, by implication, in criticizing an accepted position he felt was deficient. Like most earlier anthropologists, the study of folklore for him was integrally related to the study of custom. Literary materials, as with those derived from linguistics or from the graphic and plastic arts, were data that could be used with precision to reconstruct cultural history or to study such matters as the role of the individual in culture, the reworking of cultural materials under diffusion, and the broader questions of cultural stability and cultural change.

This is apparent in all his publications on folklore, from his first major work in the field, his important collection of Indian traditions, published in 1895 under the title *Indianische Sagen von der Nord-Pacifischen Küste Nordamerikas,* to one of his last, his only theoretical discusion of the subject, that appeared in 1938 as a chapter in his *General Anthropology.* In the first he was concerned with the problem of whether similarities between the customs, in this case the myths, of different tribes, are due to independent invention or to borrowing. Carefully tracing the form in which myth after myth is encountered in the various tribes of the Northwest Coast, he was able to trace a process of gradual change from one to the other that yielded objective and irrefutable proof of dissemination. He recognized, of course, that similarities of a broad general character, to be found everywhere in the myths and tales of peoples over the world, may be "closely connected with the emotional life of man, . . . (and) . . . are undoubtedly due to the organization of the human mind" whose "domain is large and of high importance," as he put it in the article in the *Journal of American Folk-Lore* in which he summarized these same findings. But what the analysis of the literary forms of the Northwest Coast also showed, however, was that, though "in many cases, the final decision will be in favor of independent origin; in others in favor of dissemination . . . nobody has as yet proven where the limit between these two modes of origin lies, and not until this is done can a fruitful psychological analysis take place."

In 1916 his intensive study of Tsimshian mythology appeared. This is the work for which he is perhaps best known in this field. His approach was entirely fresh, one that at that time was scarcely touched on in the analysis of written literary forms by critics and students of literary history, let alone by folklorists. What he attempted was to determine how the literature of this people reflected their life. The tales in the collection were recorded by Henry Tate, "in Tsimshian, his native language"; the translation, by Boas, was "based on a free interlinear rendering by Mr. Tate." The theoretical point, that like so many of his others that has come to be accepted as a truism, was also, like many of these others, buried in the depths of the bulky volume. "It is obvious that in the tales of a people," as he puts it on page 393, "those incidents of the everyday life that are of importance to them will appear either incidentally or as the basis of a plot. Most of the references to the mode of life of the people will be an accurate reflection of their habits. The development of the plot of the story, furthermore, will, on the whole, exhibit clearly what is considered right and what wrong." This reflection of a culture, however, is not the equivalent of a scientific ethnographic description, any more than myth can be considered as the equivalent of written history. But, as Boas says in one of his most concise phrasings, ". . . it has the merit of bringing out those points which are of interest to the people themselves. They present in a way an autobiography of the tribe."

His treatment of mythology at once brings to mind the controversy among the literary critics as to whether or not myth is the validation of belief or the expression of certain transcendental, supra-cultural and even primal symbolisms. The methodological

point at issue here is of immediate importance, especially when
it is realized that most of those who hold for the symbolic significance of myth confine their documentation to the Greek and
Roman systems, and confessedly have abstained from analyzing,
and in many cases even reading the collections from the many
parts of the world that are available to them.

Boas sets a different, and, from the point of view of induction, a more acceptable approach to the nature of myth when, in
this same work on Tsimshian mythology, he relates it, as he does
all cultural phenomena, to the larger whole of which it is a part.
He first points out that the Tsimshian "distinguish clearly between
two types of stories—the myth (*adáox*) and the tale (*mátEsk*).
The latter is entirely historical in character . . . the incidents
in the former are believed to have happened during the time when
animals appeared in the form of human beings." Indicating that
these distinctions apply to all the other tribes of the Pacific Northwest, he concludes that this "objective definition of myth" is pref-
erable for his purpose to "any of the many definitions based
on a subjective standpoint." The sentence that follows is especially
pertinent: "If it should be objected that by doing so I extend my
inquiry over and beyond the domain of myths, as defined by
various groups of investigators, I may point out that I am discussing tales which at the present time form a unit in the mind of
the Tsimshian, and that this justifies their treatment as an objective unit."

It is apparent, from Boas' later writings on the subject, that
his empirical approach to the nature of myth was not far removed
from the definition which came into currency after his death, and
holds myth to be any explanation of a way of life, or a phase of it,
that validates belief or behavior. He stressed again and again the
caution that the concept must always be held flexible. Thus he
begins the chapter entitled "Mythology and Folk-lore" in his
General Anthropology with the statement, "It is impossible to
draw a sharp line between myths and folktales. . . . ." On the
other hand, he feels it to be "fairly clear" that "stories are un-
hesitatingly classed as myths if they account for the orign of the
world and if they may be said to have happened in a mythical
period, different from the one in which we now live," a difference

recognized "by many tribes" in various parts of the world. In its organization no less than its context, mythology reflects the nature of the cultural life out of which it flows and of which it is a part. "Each particular mythology," we are told, "has its own character according to the cultural interests of the tribe."

It was unthinkable, given Boas' point of view, that a myth might be explainable in terms of any set of extra-cultural symbols. He would in conversation make sport of assertions by doctrinaire Freudians that totem-poles were sex symbols, while the concept of the racial unconscious as developed by Jung as an explanation of the resemblances in different systems of mythology he dismissed as sheer mysticism. Yet the methodological point he applied here was a general one; he was as skeptical of the symbolisms of Ehrenreich or Frobenius, who explained myth in terms of moon and sun, as he was of the system of the psychoanalysts.

So strong was his set against any explanation of symbolism except on the level of explicit cultural interpretation that he cut himself off from certain insights a cross-cultural application of such a concept as that of the unconscious might yield. Work that has been done since his death strengthens his position as to the lack of validity of symbols drawn in terms of universal equivalents. But it has also become apparent that if considered within the rubric of the culture, the analysis of unconscious symbols can be carried on with very real profit. Nor can the question of the broader validity of certain symbols, that can conceivably arise from common reactions of man to certain constants in human experience, be dismissed as summarily as Boas was wont to dismiss it.

One can understand his reactions, and need go no further than the validity of his protest against violations of basic canons of scientific method to make the point. Yet, as Boas himself recognized in the study of conventionalizations in art, for example, intra-cultural symbolisms do exist. Perhaps the pendulum will have again to settle to its center, so that the position of both the extreme symbolists and of those who have rejected this point of view may be tested by inductions from the data of many cultures. On this basis only will conclusions be drawn that will profit both from the insights of a Freud and the methodological cautions of a Boas.

4

It might be thought that the students of literature who have been concerned with the nature of myth would logically have turned some of their interest to the analysis of the myths they study. But they have not done so; indeed, except for Boas and a handful of his students, this approach to folktale and mythology is over almost entirely unexplored terrain.

When we seek the reason for this, we again sound the refrain that has been encountered so frequently in the preceding pages, that for Boas, the phenomena of culture were always treated as reflexes of the thoughts and actions of human beings. Thus for him, myths and tales, as the phrase goes, could never "lie flat in the ethnographer's notebook." Unlike those whose analysis of "primitive" stories was confined to the study, rather than taken into the field, he knew at first-hand the artistry in the telling of these unwritten literary forms and how it is a part of the creative process that has brought myth and tale and poem into being.

As for the many anthropologists who have been in the field, and have heard the tales told, the myths recounted, the songs sung, have they, too, not experienced this artistry? And, if so, why have most of them failed to sense these artistic values? The question does not permit of a simple answer, but the probability is that the explanation lies in the fact that their emphases have been on the institutional aspects of the life with which they have been concerned or, at the other extreme, on the individual as he reacts to his culture. Neither is conducive to the overview that comes from studying a way of life, as manifested in individual responses, as a unit, of the sort that Boas preached and practiced; for it is from such an overview alone that the subtleties of the creative effort can be perceived, analyzed, and thus deepen our understanding of the life of man in general.

Boas phrased this aspect of his approach to unwritten literature in a number of articles, but it is perhaps best expressed in the chapter—"Mythology and Folklore" in his *General Anthro-*

pology. A myth, he stated, "cannot be understood solely as a result of speculative thought about the origin and structure of the world and of human life. It is no less an outflow of artistic, more specifically literary activity." As for folk-tales, these "must be considered as analogous to modern novelistic literature. . . . The free play of imagination operating with everyday experiences is sufficient to account for their origin." The question why a given individual, in a given culture, manifests this "free play" of the imagination and another apparently does not, Boas never faced. When answers to it were suggested, as by the psychoanalysts, he firmly rejected them, in consonance with his general attitude toward explanations of this order.

Rather he struck a balance between two approaches to exotic arts that, through the influence exerted by his writings and those of his students, has done much to bring the discussion of such art-forms of all kinds into perspective. On the one hand, as we have seen, in refusing to consider "primitive" man as an undeveloped, child-like creature, he rejected the point of those who held the literature, the carving, the painting of "primitive" peoples to be crude efforts from the childhood of man. The equation which places the paintings of "modern" children in direct comparison with the art of "primitive" adults, a formulation that was developing during his later years, brought forth withering comment from him. On the other hand, he rejected with equal vigor the ecstatic phrasings of the art critics, especially those dealing with the graphic and plastic arts, who saw in the art of "primitive" man exotic, mystical manifestations of some deep instinctual urge, to be regarded with awe, and understood but dimly by "civilized" man as he responds from his deepest being to this thing he can never intellectually comprehend. By reducing these art-forms to the proportion of creations of individual artists, working within the frame of their own cultures, he opened the way to reach depths of understanding of the creative process and aesthetic response that have been little recognized, much less exploited, since he wrote.

Boas' studies of the nature of art and literature and the settings under which they are created would undoubtedly have had greater influence on literary and art criticism in general if his discussion had not been essentially that of the anthropologist, and thus not keyed to the conventions of literary and art criticism, or the style of art history. It is obvious, in reading him, moreover, that his vocabulary did not equal his perceptions; the reader accustomed to the literary quality of critical writing must be willing to cope with stylistic inadequacies if he is to profit from the very real insights to be gained from its fresh ideas. Consider, for example, a passage that introduces the concluding chapter of his *Primitive Art,* where he sets forth his concept of the nature of art: "We have seen that art arises from two sources, from technical pursuits and from the expression of emotions and thought as soon as these take fixed forms. The more energetic the control of form over uncoordinated movement, the more esthetic the result. Artistic enjoyment is, therefore, based essentially upon the reaction of our minds to form."

It is apparent if one will study this passage, that despite the phrasing, it contains a wealth of suggestion for fruitful study of the graphic and plastic arts of other societies, which are so often misunderstood; when, notably as in the instance of unwritten literature, their artistry has not been entirely ignored. Boas treated the latter in various discussions, shaping his ideas first in an article he published in 1925 in Germany and, two years later in the United States, and which he also included in his volume of collected papers, "Stylistic Aspects of Primitive Literature." Here he is obviously feeling his way. The methodological difficulty of obtaining adequate textual materials, validly translated, troubles him. His digressions to consider matters quite extraneous to his topic, such as the geographical distributions of particular types of literary forms, and the bearing these have on such essentially anthropological questions as the historical development of each type and their possible relation to the race of those who developed them, also reflect the newness of the question for him.

Some of these digressions are present in the chapter on literature, music and dance Boas wrote ten years later for his general textbook, but here they have a minor place; his ideas have by now taken on definite form and sharper delineation. Some of the generalizations he advances, it is true, have been negated by work done since his time. Thus, it does not follow that because a people live near the subsistence level, their art is in the main restricted to tales, music and dance. We have learned that the Australian aborigines, whom he cites as a case in point, number among them artists who paint on bark, while he overlooked the world-famous polychrome paintings of the South African Bushmen, who also are such a marginal people.

Nonetheless, his discussion of literary forms and their relation to music and dance are full of significant and stimulating observations. The fact that poetry, in most nonliterate societies, takes the form of words to songs, and through this has the most intimate relation to the dance, points an association whose implications for the analysis of rhythm in all these modes of expression have still to be probed. Repetition of words or phrases as a device to increase tension is documented with examples from Hawaii, from New Zealand, from the Eskimo and the Kwakiutl Indians. The richness of the imagery in the poetry of nonliterate peoples, as expressed in their use of metaphor, the example he uses, is similarly pointed.

"The form of modern prose," Boas suggests, with great insight, "is largely determined by the fact that it is read, not spoken, while primitive prose is based on the art of oral delivery," this being a factor of importance in making for the "considerable . . . stylistic difference between the two." As for the way in which the structure of the tales of nonliterate peoples is shaped, Boas was one of the first to point out that the play of "free elements," the incidents of a story, which had long been noted and studied for their distributional variation, also reflect "the taste and ability of the narrator." And it brings the creative factor in literary expression among nonliterate folk to familiar human terms when we read, in Boas' chapter on literature in *Primitive Art*, that "poetic susceptibility is not the same everywhere, neither in form nor in intensity. The local culture determines what kind of experiences have a poetic value and the intensity with which they act."

Unlike the interest Boas had in analyzing the oral arts of nonliterate peoples as literature, which developed late in his career, his concern with the graphic and plastic arts is to be traced to his earliest research. There can be little doubt that his ideas on the relation between "technical virtuosity and the fullness of artistic development," a theme basic to his discussion, derives from his observations among the Eskimo. The study he later made of the decorative designs of Alaskan Eskimo needle-cases not only tested the prevailing theories as to the origin of conventionalization in art and its relationship to realism, but made an important positive contribution. It was here that he pointed out how, in these objects, the decorative embellishments, consisting both of geometric designs and of realistic representations of seals, are the result of the play of the imagination of the Eskimo artist who carves them, in terms of prevalent patterns, on the "small knobs or the flanges" that hold the lashings about them in place. As a result, "after this modification has once set in, the animal figures may be represented on other parts of the implement," a treatment that is encouraged by the fact that, in addition, "the old form or style of the needlecase determined the treatment of the animal form."

Even before he made his study, Boas had worked at his remarkable analysis of the art of the Northwest Coast Indians, based on his researches in the field. This was probably the first study in which the range of artistic expression in a nonliterate society was recognized, and provided an interpretation of patterns of conventionalization not on the basis of the deductions of the art form by the student, but on that of the explanation provided by the people themselves. The relation between form and medium, a question much debated in later years, is pointed here by the fact that the shape of Northwest Coast totem-poles is "limited by the cylindrical form of the trunk of the tree from which they are carved." He also showed that in this culture—and later, as he found, in others—there are differences in the art styles of men and of women, a point of considerable importance when we realize how often "the" art of a people is described without taking this into account. He further demonstrated that, contrary to what assumptions as to the unity of "primitive" culture would require, among these people "realistic representations are not beyond the powers of the artist," despite the predominant conventionalizations of their art. The bulk of this discussion, however, is given over to a painstaking analysis of motif after motif, until the complex distortions for which Northwest Coast art has become famous are laid bare and their symbolisms revealed. It is understandable that this study has for years been a model after which comparable analyses of the art of other peoples by anthropologists have been made.

An invitation from the Institute for the Comparative Study of Culture, in Oslo, to deliver a series of lectures made it possible for Boas to assemble his ideas and data on primitive art and publish them in its distinguished series of reports. Here he was able, at length, and with ample illustrations, to develop his discussions of questions that had occupied him for so many years —the importance of the formal elements in art, and their varied manifestations; the determinants and forms of representative and stylized expressions of art; the factors that enter into the determination of art style and make for stability and change in an art. Not only this, but the scope of the work permitted him to bring oral and musical arts into his discussion.

As always, the pertinent theoretical anthropological problems are considered. The question of unilateral evolution, of historic transmission, of art as an element in culture, of the role of the individual as manifested in the personal expression of the creative artist, the limitations imposed on his creativeness by the concept of beauty held by his people—these are also given full and formal treatment. Some of the questions asked by art-students are raised—the relation between form and function in art, between medium and mode of treatment, and, inevitably, the character and significance of symbolism.

As in all Boas' writings, here we find induction, breadth of interest, the humanistic approach. We are shown how art, in any of its forms, springs from the creativeness of the individual, shaped, but never entirely contained, by the pattern of a culture. Its reward for the artist in any society we clearly see to be twofold—the satisfactions the virtuoso obtains from his own achievement, and from the appreciation accorded him by his fellows.

5

Boas never enunciated the philosophical principles that guided his approach to the nature of man and of human culture, since speculation, as such, did not appeal to him. The philosophical implications of evolutionism offer a case in point, since here the concept of progress figures intimately and presents problems of ultimate values that call for resolution. As conceived by the evolutionists, the idea of progress interpreted the fact of change, which all recognized, so that it became directed change, from what was held to be less desired to that which was regarded as more desirable. In the study of biological evolution, this was scarcely more than implicit, and eventually dropped out entirely; but in considering the presumed evolution of social and cultural phenomena, it was crucial. Moreover, since it was congenial to the thinking of those who deemed themselves the exponents of the ultimate stage of the evolutionary progression, it became firmly fixed in the constellation of sanctions that underlies European and American culture.

The problem troubled Boas, who returned to it repeatedly in his writings. One comes from these discussions with the feeling that he was struggling with a difficulty which may perhaps be expressed as follows: If each society develops in accordance with the experiences of its own historic past, and universal sequences of change from lower to higher stages of culture cannot be established by the use of the comparative method, how can the concept of progress be considered as susceptible of scientific proof?

Certainly, insofar as the doctrine meant acceptance of the principle that those differences between "primitive" and "civilized" ways of life, considered in the large and as wholes, reflected differing degrees of evolution, so that "primitve" peoples were to be regarded as retarded, child-like examples of the earlier stages through which "civilized" peoples had passed, there could be no equivocation as far as he was concerned. His experiences with the many nonliterate aggregates among whom he had lived taught him better. These people might have customs and beliefs that were different from those of Europe and America, and they might not manifest the same degree of technological complexity; but they were no children, and their cultures were no forerunners of the way of life he knew.

Yet, at the same time, Boas, like all men, was conditioned to the patterns of thought of his own culture. It was impossible for him, as a scientist, to look on science and not find it good—not only good for his society, but for mankind as a whole. The vision of the results to be obtained for humanity from the application of reason to the problems that beset man—of health, of poverty, of war, of restrictions on individual liberty—this vision moved him deeply. He was thus loath to follow through the implications of his position, which would force the admission that science is only one of a number of techniques of adjusting to the natural world, and that other techniques, in theory at least, are to be accepted as of equal worth.

His statement of the difficulty, in its most explicit form, and his resolution of it, are to be found in his *Anthropology and Modern Life*. "We may recognize progress," he says, "in a definite direction in the development of invention and knowledge. If we should value a society entirely on the basis of its technical and scientific achievements it would be easy to establish a line of progress which, although not uniform, leads from simplicity to complexity. Other aspects of cultural life are not with equal ease brought into a progressive sequence."

Thus the opportunity for participation in the whole culture by all the people, found in other societies, was contrasted by him to fragmentation of our own way of life. "It is a reproach to our civilization," he points out, "that we have not learned to utilize the vastly increased leisure in the way done by primitive man." Or, commenting on the discussions by Hobhouse and Westermarck on the evolution of moral ideas, Boas says, "It might seem that the low value given to life in primitive society and the cruelty of primitive man are indications of a low ethical standard. It is quite possible to show an advance in ethical *behavior* when we compare primitive society to our own. . . . Their descriptions are quite true, but I do not believe that they represent a growth of moral *ideas,* but rather reflect the same moral ideas as manifested in different types of society and taking on forms varying according to the extent of knowledge of the people." The conclusion is a simple one: ". . . the term 'cultural progress' can be used in a restricted sense only. It refers to increase of knowledge and of control of nature." For the rest, "it is not easy to define progress in any phase of social life" other than these: "We may speak of progress in certain directions, hardly of absolute progress, except in so far as it is dependent upon knowledge which contributes to the safety of human life, health, and comfort."

The most important contribution to philosophical thought that Boas made was, as might be expected, an implicit one. It grew out of his tolerance for other ways of life than his own, a recognition of their values, and an understanding of the human misery, degradation and demoralization that can result when one people imposes its way on another. As a teacher, too, he had realized what it means to expose a student to other modes of behavior and thought than his own. He had found how this allows, and in the case of the good student compels him to look with fresh perspective at the things he has held as eternal truths and absolute ends. In the final paragraph of his *General Anthropology,* he writes of "that freedom from cultural prejudice which in itself can be attained only by the intensive study of foreign cultures of fundamentally distinctive types that make clear to us which among our own concepts are determined by our modern culture and which may be generally valid, because based on human nature."

Though Boas never explicitly formulated the philosophical implications of his methodology and his findings, there can be no doubt as to his position concerning the values in culture. In his initial paper published under the title "The Mind of Primitive Man," he points out that, "the difference in the mode of thought of primitive man and civilized man seems to consist largely in the difference of character of the traditional material with which the new perception associates itself." Ten years later, in discussing "Psychological Problems in Anthropology," he lays down the principle that "one of the fundamental points to be borne in mind in the development of anthropological psychology is the necessity of looking for the common psychological features, not in the outward similarities of ethnic phenomena, but in the similarity of psychological processes so far as these can be observed or inferred."

The vast body of materials that anthropologists, over the past fifty years, have collected has given sound support to the proposition that each society, in resolving its own problems in its own manner, attaches values to its own procedures that for its members are beyond question. Moreover, it has come to be realized that because all value-judgments are culture-bound, evaluation across cultural lines must allow for the factors of ethnocentric orientation. "It is somewhat difficult for us to recognize that the value which we attribute to our own civilization is due to the fact that we participate in this civilization, and that it has been controlling all our actions since the time of our birth"; he wrote, "but it is certainly conceivable that there may be other civilizations, based perhaps on different traditions and on different equilibrium of emotion and reason which are of no less value than ours, although it may be impossible for us to appreciate their influence. The general theory of valuation of human activities, as developed by anthropological research, teaches us a higher tolerance than the one we now profess."

From the point of view of scientific induction, it has become apparent, as it was to Boas, that because there are universals in human experience, this does not mean that the absolute value attached by any particular cultural group to any particular cultural manifestation of a universal is valid for any other. This philosophy of cultural relativism, as it is called, thus stems from the documentation of custom and a theory of the unity of mankind, toward which Boas made an outstanding contribution.

CHAPTER FIVE

THE SCIENTIST AS CITIZEN

WHEN Boas assumed the professorship at Columbia University he was to hold for almost fifty years, the ivory tower stood remote from the workaday world. The support society gave the scholar derived from a conviction that, in the long run, the people as a whole would profit from his findings, however esoteric his investigations, or however difficult it might be to tell just what form this profit would take. It seemed almost an article of faith that, given time and patience, material benefits, or gains in the adjustments to life that come from a deepened comprehension of the nature of the world, would accrue to all. Such examples as the discovery of the X-ray by Roentgen were frequently cited as cases in point to justify a student's probing into any question he felt posed a problem of sufficient intellectual challenge to deserve his time and effort.

As the years passed, however, a more immediate relevance of research to approved objectives began to be stressed. With an initial impulse from such obvious areas of research as medicine, agriculture, and industrial chemistry, it moved, under the impact of the Second World War, to the exact and natural sciences, the social sciences and, later, even came to afford criteria for evaluating proposals for research in the humanistic disciplines. The demands of this fast-moving period of history, in the United States, at least, were strengthened by an established pragmatic point of view. This complex of attitudes forced the scholar increasingly into the current of everyday affairs, causing more and more investigators to depart from their earlier aim of fulfilling what has been termed the curiosity of function of scholarship, and devote themselves to the analysis of specific problems raised by practical needs.

Boas moved with the times and with his discipline; but, as far as anthropology was concerned, the times moved slowly. Until after the First World War, anthropologists studied with scholarly detachment the basic questions that were to provide the theoretical and conceptual foundations of their science. During this period, it was other disciplines which were on the firing-line of public controversy, or under pressure to apply their findings to matters of immediate concern. For a long time it was biology, whose theory of evolution came under attack; in the social sciences, the demand that economics, political science and sociology be applied to contemporary questions was continuous. Technology was moving to join with, and eventually almost to blanket, pure research in the exact sciences.

The turn of anthropologists to defend their position came between the two World Wars when, with the rise of the Nazis in Germany, the scientific concept of race was perverted to provide authority for a virulent racism that aimed at prostituting anthropology for political ends. The drive for the application of the techniques and data of ethnology and linguistics to current problems developed with the increase in rapidity of communications during the Second World War and after. It was only then that the potential contribution of these branches of the science toward understanding the diverse modes of belief and behavior with which any world Power must deal, and to which it must adjust policy and program if a degree of amity is to be attained, became patent.

The problem posed by the invasion of the ivory tower brought the scientist face to face with questions that go beyond the scope of scientific analysis, since they can be resolved only in terms of ethical values. How, indeed, is the obligation of the scholar to the society that supports him to be discharged? What if certain results of the findings of long-term programs of research, as seen from the point of view of their relation to ultimate ends, turn out to be harmful, rather than of positive worth? Or, as is more often the case, what should be the course of the scientist when he finds that his discovery can be pointed either toward goals of which he approves, or toward those he believes undesirable? The dilemma of the nuclear physicists comes immediately to mind, but their difficulty differs only from those in other disciplines in the dramatic quality of the potentialities of their discoveries for the conquest of natural forces, or at the same time for the destruction of human beings and the very achievements their researches have brought within reach.

Anthropologists have no more been able to escape this dilemma than other scientists. From the very beginning of systematic research on the differences between human groups, physical anthropology has been plagued by the rationalizations for racism it provided. In the United States, the work of the early scientists in the field figured prominently in the mid-Nineteenth Century controversy between the abolitionists and the proponents of slavery. In the hands of those who followed the theories of Count Gobineau and Houston Stewart Chamberlain, the formula for the cephalic index, a simple device to further the quantitative analysis of differences in physical type, was transmuted into a qualitative expression to designate a presumably superior "race," first called Teutonic, then Nordic, and still later Aryan. Later, the ethnologist, with his techniques of probing through outer cultural form to inner sanction in societies other than his own, was forced to face the fact that the manipulation of the way of life of a people can bring on demoralization even where material well-being is enhanced. Thus as a scientist, the anthropologist studies his problem and publishes his results. With other scientists, he seeks the answer to this basic ethical problem, as yet unsolved, of how to ensure that his findings are used by those who would direct them toward ends inimical to the canons of morality of the scientific tradition within which he works.

Boas' approach to the problem was consistent. Two fundamental ideas can be traced throughout the course of his professional life. One was that the scientist must be free to pursue his investigations wherever the data lead him, to reach his conclusions with regard only for the principles of scientific method as they apply to these data, and to publish his conclusions without hindrance, subject only to critical testing by his fellow-scientists. The second concerned the duty of the scientist to ensure that these results would not be irresponsibly used, by sharing his findings with the public that supports him, making them known and understood by his fellow-citizens through the use of every means at his command.

Long before the problem of the uses to which the findings of scientists might be put had become acute, when it was not seriously questioned that the power knowledge gave would be for good, it will be remembered that Boas insisted museum displays "impart systematic information" to those who came to them for "healthy entertainment and instruction." His dictum, already quoted, that "every kind of inaccuracy should be most carefully avoided, and attempts to make all problems appear childish simply by the elimination of everything that is obscure should not be tolerated," indicates how, as early as 1907, he made explicit his concept of the duty of the scholar toward what might be termed his constituency.

The "Introduction" to a posthumous volume entitled *Race and Democratic Society,* for which, prior to his death, Boas collected some of his more important lay addresses, is given over to the text of a statement broadcast internationally on September 27, 1941, during a Conference on Science and the World Order held by the British Association for the Advancement of Science. Since the broadcast occurred a little more than a year before his death, this statement is to be regarded as the definitive enunciation of his position on the problem of the scientist as citizen.

"Who among us," he began his broadcast, "when trying to solve some theoretical problem, has not felt some time or other that his problems are puny and irrelevant when the whole world is aflame, when millions are dying by the sword, by bombs, by starvation? Who has not felt the irresistible urge to do his share in the defense of freedom, in the battle waged for saving our intellectural integrity from the domineering spirit that would fetter the freedom of thought by subjecting it to the control of prescribed opinion?" The question thus stated, Boas, after posing the difficulty of deciding "whether it is our duty to lay aside our studies for the time being and enter heart and soul the battle for democracy and intellectual freedom," gives his reply in unyielding terms.

"It seems to me," he wrote, "that there is only one possible answer to this question. We cannot give up our work as scientists without irreparable damage to our culture, no matter how remote our subject may be from the urgent, practical needs of our time. The ice-cold flame of the passion for seeking the truth for truth's sake must be kept burning and can be kept alive only if we continue to seek the truth for truth's sake."

This, however, is not all. The same feeling that in 1907 caused him to insist on the duty of a museum to educate the citizen is apparent in his conception of the obligation which is the other side of the scientist's coin whose obverse is the privilege of freedom of research and publication. "We must see to it that the hard task of subordinating the love of traditional lore to clear thinking must be shared with us by larger and larger masses of our people. . . . It is not the spread of a superficial knowledge of the results of science that will accomplish this end. We must do our share in the task of weaning the people from a complacent yielding to prejudice, and help them to the power of clear thought, that they may be able to understand the problems that confront all of us."

Boas, speaking at the height of a war against authoritarianism, draws the lesson for those who would preserve the tradition of freedom of thought in an enlightened democratic system. "A people, so educated, will be free in the fullest sense of the term. It will more nearly approach the ideal of democracy than has been attained by any of us." He might here have added still another article of faith by which he lived—that a people, so educated, will be the best assurance that the powerful instruments, physical and social, the scientist places in the hands of those charged with the determination and implementation of policy will be used in accordance with the constructive purposes for which, in the view of scientists as men of good will, they are intended.

2

Boas was one of the first to attempt to apply anthropological findings to problems of the day. Well before the turn of the century, he was studying the growth of children with the end in view of ascertaining the normal patterns of development in height and weight, two of the best indicators of physical well-being of the child. In the "head-form" study, again, he put his knowledge at the disposal of the Senate Committee concerned with the question of immigration. Though the scientific results proved more important than any directions for practical procedures which issued from the research, this was not because the investigation was not pointed toward questions under public debate.

His views on the practical implications of cultural anthropology were first presented in 1928, also early, as such things go, when his book, *Anthropology and Modern Life,* first appeared. It was a distinct departure in the literature of his discipline, but the fact that a revised edition was brought out in 1932 indicates that it filled an actual need. In the preface to the revision, he tells in a sentence the role he felt his science could play in making for better understanding of common problems of the day. "In writing the present book," he states, "I desired to show that some of the most firmly rooted opinions of our times appear from a wider point of view as prejudices, and that a knowledge of anthropology enables us to look with greater freedom at the problems confronting our civilization."

To this end, he considered, as we might expect, the nature of race and the interrelation of races, and the forms and functioning of culture, especially as the matter of conformity and nonconformity to prevailing patterns bears on the problem of cultural stability, and as a knowledge of culture holds significance for educational practices. It is of some interest, however, that he also went outside these customary topics of his interest, to treat of questions of nationalism, eugenics and criminology. The basis for the sense of nationalism, we are told, lies in linguistic, cultural and physical uniformities that, as we move from tribal to ever larger territorial units, present the dangers of ever more powerful aggressive drives for conquest and rule. His discussion of eugenics stressed from the need to distinguish between inborn and learned aptitudes and drives, and cautioned against attempting to solve what are essentially culturally determined problems by invoking mechanisms of biological control. As for the problem of the criminal, he emphasized its essentially cultural—or "environ-

mental" nature, as he termed it—as against the attribution of
innate anti-social predispositions in those who violate the law.

His approach to practical problems was thus broad, drawn
in terms of the aid an understanding of anthropological fact and
theory can provide those charged with their solution. This point
of view was adumbrated in his writings as early as 1899, when he
urged that anthropology be included in the curriculum of the
undergraduate, "because it extends his view over cultures and
civilizations that have grown up uninfluenced by our own." Much
later, in 1940, in prefacing the collection of his scientific papers,
he repeated this same sentiment: "Growing up in our civilization
we know little how we ourselves are conditioned by it, how our
bodies, our language, our modes of thinking and acting are determined by limits imposed on us by our environment. Knowledge
of the life processes and behavior of man under conditions of life
fundamentally different from our own can help us to obtain a
freer view of our own lives and of our own problems."

Insofar as cultural anthropology is concerned, Boas never
went on to point out what have come to be commonplace applications of ethnology to quite specific problems. That anthropologists might undertake such tasks as analyzing situations where
peoples having differing bodies of tradition come into contact,
with a view of anticipating and avoiding tension, or suggesting
modes of resolving cross-cultural conflicts where these may have
arisen—to say nothing of studying how proposed innovations in
the ethnologist's own culture might be brought in line with pre-
existing patterns—these were not envisaged in his writings.

The fact is, that in Boas' day cultural anthropology lacked
the theoretical and methodological competence to cope with
questions of this order. Among other things, their study involves
assessing cultural change on the basis of comparing data derived
from different periods in the history of a given people. We cannot
ascribe prevision to the students of culture who emphasized the
importance of recovering the historic past of the tribal groups
they studied, describing a culture as it no longer existed rather
than analyzing what was often the pathological situation of social
demoralization in the mist of which their investigations were actually carried on. Yet those who rail at them for devoting themselves

to the reconstructed past rather than the observed present show an absence of historic sense. For without the record of aboriginal civilizations in their earlier, relatively undisturbed state, it would be impossible today to grasp the extensiveness and significance of the changes that have taken place as a result of contact with other peoples.

Though the applicability of anthropological techniques to the great literate societies is by no means a matter of agreement, the utility of an ethnological approach where cross-cultural factors are involved has come generally to be recognized. More specifically, its utility has become self-evident where industrialized, literate societies and small, nonliterate groupings, subsumed under the earlier designation "primitive," are in contact. In the Americas, this has meant giving attention to what is called the "Indian problem." In Europe, it has implied utilizing anthropological knowledge in attempts to solve practical questions of colonial administration.

During most of Boas' lifetime, however—actually, until about a decade before his death—even when such ideas were advanced, as they sometimes were, any discussion of them was of necessity academic, since there were so few anthropologists that the problem of securing adequately trained men and women to carry on tasks of this sort was insurmountable. Teaching and research, in universities and natural history museums, were the objectives toward which all training was pointed. Any attention an anthropologist cared to give to the solution of such practical issues as he felt he might aid in resolving was strictly his own affair, and, insofar as his professional obligations were concerned, was entirely extracurricular.

One might summarize Boas' applications of anthropology to the problems of the day by stating that they were essentially pedagogical. His approach was fundamentally that of the research scientist. The assumptions on which social action was predicated were stated, put to the test of scientific scrutiny, their degree of validity noted, and the readjustments implied by the findings indicated. How any changes suggested were to be implemented, however, was for the practical man to decide. The role played by the scientist was that of the astronomer charting the stars, not

that of the navigator, who used the knowledge thus provided to
guide his vessel.

3

Boas early became concerned over the situation of the Negro
in the United States. His contribution to the solution of what is
termed the "race problem," in accordance with his customary
practice, consisted entirely of fundamental background materials,
and consequently his discussions take two forms, and only two.
One has to do with the extent to which the particular traits of
Negroes that at the time were held to make them second-class
participants in American culture were validly to be ascribed to
innate causes, or were the result of the social and economic setting
of their lives. The second was even more remote from the issues
of the moment. It took the form of pointing out the complex
nature of African culture, and from this drawing the lesson that,
contrary to beliefs widely held, the ancestors of the American
Negro manifested ability of a high order for cultural achievement, and that the expectancy of achievement of the Negro in
the United States, given opportunity to achieve, was equal to that
for any other group in the population.

An article entitled "Industries of the African Negroes" which
Boas published in 1909 in *The Southern Workman,* a periodical
brought out by Hampton Institute, typifies his approach. Its opening sentence clearly states the point at issue: "Our judgment of
the abilities of the black race is determined by our knowledge of
the Negro in North America; and the principal fact that impresses
itself upon our minds is the backwardness, inertia, and lack of
initiative, of the great masses in the South, which cannot be out-
weighed by the achievements of exceptional individuals but by
the slow but steady progress of the race as a whole." The need
for the wider perspective of anthropological science is expressed
in these terms: "An adequate judgment of the capacities of a
whole race, based on so narrow a field of experience, is hardly
possible. . . . Nothing that may be observed in our country can
show what the capacities of the race may be in other surroundings; a broader treatment of the question will require a considera-

tion of the achievements of the Negro under other conditions, and particularly of the culture that he has developed in his own natural surroundings." In Africa, he points out, we find industriousness, application to the task in hand, order, organization. At this early date, too, he recognized the "artistic merit" of the African, to which "unfortunately our American museums have never paid any adequate attention . . ., although we ought to recognize that a knowledge of the African at home would help us materially in the solution of our Negro problem."

It was this same theme that had dominated his Commencement Address at Atlanta University in 1906, though in this case his approach was influenced by the nature of his audience. "The fundamental requirement," the graduates must meet if they were to "be fitted to fill" their "place in the life of the nation," he said, was "a clear insight into the capabilities of your own race." The discovery of iron-working in Africa, the existence of great kingdoms in the continent, the native system of law-courts, are detailed to the end that "to those who stoutly maintain a material inferiority of the Negro race and who would dampen your ardor by their claims, you may confidently reply that the burden of proof rests with them, that the past history of your race does not sustain their statement, but rather gives you encouragement." And he added, "You may . . . say that you have set out to recover for the colored people the strength that was their own before they set foot on the shores of this continent."

It was only in later years that Boas expressed himself concerning the future of the Negro, but his conclusions were again drawn in general terms: "If my view is correct," he wrote in 1921, "it is clear that the only fundamental remedy for the situation is the recognition that Negroes have the right to be treated as individuals, not as members of a class." That this was within the range of practical achievement seemed to him most unlikely. "How can this be brought about in a population that is so deeply saturated with class consciousness as our own?" Education might help, but it would have to combat the emotional ties that are established in the individual to hold him to the group with which he identifies himself, and would be a long road. "There is no great hope that the Negro problem will find even a half-way satisfactory solution in our day." With deep pessimism, he concluded, "It would seem that man being what he is, the Negro problem will not disappear in America until the Negro blood has been so much diluted that it will no longer be recognized just as anti-Semitism will not disappear until the last vestige of the Jew as a Jew has disappeared."

Boas, however, prescribed better than he predicted. The pressures of the Second World War and post-war years toward the implementation of democratic professions in the field of American race relations have operated continuously against those who would stand for segregation, lack of economic and social opportunity and denial of political rights to minority groups. The full acceptance of the Negro as a fellow citizen and fellow member of the community remains to be achieved, but gains have been made toward that end which Boas would never have dreamed possible. And in achieving this much, the broad general approach toward the questions of race and cultural aptitude urged by him over the years as providing the conceptual and factual basis for implementing more equable human relations, exerting the quiet, constant intellectual pressure of scientific truth, has in no small measure been responsible for directing this trend.

The areas wherein the application of anthropology to practical questions has come to be most recognized—problems of dependent peoples and, particularly in the Americas, of the Indian —Boas treated only in passing, if at all. Matters of colonial rule touched him lightly. This is understandable, since he never conducted research in any area of European dominance; like most Americans, he regarded Puerto Rico, where he took physical measurements, as a "possession" and not a colony. It is understandable, too, because the colonial problem did not become acute until shortly before his death, the dependency of colonial peoples being more or less taken for granted during his lifetime. As a Nineteenth Century liberal, he rejected, in principle, the colonial system. But as a Nineteenth Century liberal with a European orientation, he tended to think in terms of the needs of Europe, even though without enthusiasm where colonialism was concerned. The conclusion he reached in 1915, on one of the few occasions when he discussed the subject, reflects the conflict inherent in his doubly oriented position: "I presume the desire of each nationality to find an adequate field for her own activities can never be overcome so long as we have expanding nations speaking different languages and having different individualities; and therefore we have to make the best of it."

As regards the Indian, there is no doubt where his sympathies lay, for his reactions to American and Canadian policy were strong. He had witnessed at first-hand the social tragedies that were continuously being enacted as a result of the application to these helpless groups of governmental policies conceived without cultural understanding and executed with disregard for their effect on the personality of those subject to them. He would frequently express his concern over such policies, citing as a case in point the demoralizing effect on the Kwakiutl, among whom he had lived and worked, of the rigorous suppression of the potlatch, the give-away that was a crucial factor in their way of life, and the listlessness and demoralization that resulted. One of his few published expressions on Indian policy, indeed, is found in a letter protesting against the severe laws drawn against potlatching, and published in a *Bulletin* of the Eastern Association on Indian Affairs in 1924.

There were some who, despite the apparent hopelessness of the situation, waged a continuous up-hill battle in behalf of the Indian. Like most of his fellow-anthropologists, however, Boas, though entirely sympathetic to their endeavors, was not active in prosecuting the cause. The force of the frontier tradition was, in actuality, still too great to permit effective action through mobilizing public opinion; and if the anthropologists did not phrase their position in this way, the hopeless shrug of the shoulders that at this period greeted suggestions that action be initiated to remedy the damage already done and stay further attack on Indian culture and self-respect showed that their sense of political impotence was very real.

There is another explanation for Boas' abstention from active participation in the movement for Indian rights. In the case of prejudice against the Negroes and the Jews, the resulting tensions arose out of the ascription of innate, racial characteristics as the cause of real or supposed social inadequacy or deviation. The Indian was accused of many deficiencies, but the tradition of the noble Redskin was nonetheless strong, and acted as a barrier to charges of innate, racial inferiority, as against cultural failings. Boas' discussions of the problems of minority groups, however, brings just this ascription of innate, racial tendencies under fire. This does not mean that in his theoretical approach to cultural differences, he admitted any claim of innate inferiority as regards any people, no matter how simple their mode of life might seem. Yet the consistent contrast he drew in his writing between "primitive" nonliterate, and historic societies, suggests that he never resolved for himself the question of values involved in comparing these types of civilizations, certainly not to any degree approaching the clarity of his resolution of the question of racial differences in endowment.

Perhaps the matter may be expressed in these terms: Where physical characteristics were concerned, and the question of the relation between race and culture was raised, his terms of reference were precise, and his mastery of implication complete. In contrast, in evaluating cultural differences, his human approach and broad tolerance, derived from the code of Nineteenth Century liberalism that so influenced his every attitude, came into conflict with his devotion to the values of his own culture inculcated in him through his early training and the experiences of the years of his early manhood.

Whatever the case, when the call for cooperation with those charged with administering Indian affairs was heard, so that anthropologists might aid in halting demoralization and hastening readjustment to the situation as it existed in the mid-nineteen-thirties, other practical problems pressed too hard on Boas, and he left the task to younger men. For this turn in the official approach toward the Indian came at the precise moment of the rise of Hitler and Nazi racism in Germany; and this world tragedy, for Boas, with his years of combatting the myth of racial superiority behind him, had obviously to take precedence over all lesser issues. More than any other, it summoned him yet again to bring to bear all the prestige and intellectual power his preeminence in the scientific study of race could mobilize, to aid in staying the spread of this recrudescence of racial bigotry, and to make his contribution to its ultimate defeat.

4

Those who question the values and goals of their society, and urge alternatives to accepted action, for the most part voice their dissent in the early years of their maturity. The rebel is typically the young man or woman; but the prognosis points to a dissolution of discontent with the passing of the years. The causes for which the mellowed liberal contended in his youth become the conventions of later years, which in turn confront the oncoming generation, for whom they represent the established order.

Boas was a striking exception to this rule. There is nothing in his earlier writings to indicate any unusual concern with economic or political questions. He hewed narrowly to the line of his scientific research, except perhaps for his discussions of the place of the Negro in American society, which themselves were essentially applications of established facts to a situation where the best interests of all was to order behavior in accordance with these facts. One of his earliest publications on a subject of general political interest, entitled "An Anthropologist's View of War," conforms to this pattern. Written in 1912, when he was over fifty years of age, it is a reasoned documentation of his convictions as a pacifist. In it, he sketches, in scholarly terms, the development of minute tribal entities into ever larger population aggregates, and indicates how this gives hope for a warless world society; drawing the conclusion that conflicts based on aggressive nationalisms are not inevitable concomitants of a future political order.

The outbreak of the First World War was a dual challenge to him. The vast scope of the conflict, even in its earlier years, made it a necessity for him to express again and again his established conviction that war was evil. In addition to this, however, the allegations circulated in the United States against the country of his birth, whose humanistic and scientific traditions had given direction to his life, drove him to make forthright answer. Letters to the New York *Times,* the *Atlantic Monthly,* in addition to articles in various other periodicals of general circulation appear in his bibliography, urging the iniquity of war and protesting against what he regarded as unjustifiable distortions of German culture.

The participation of the United States altered the position of those who, during the period of American neutrality, had been in opposition to the dominant point of view. Calls to ferret out those who did not give complete assent to the war effort were heard from every side. The universities of the country were no more exempt from this than any other facet of American life, and dismissals of teachers from their academic posts because they were suspected of lack of enthusiasm for the cause gave rise to a number of famous cases, among the best known of which were those of Boas' colleagues, James Harvey Robinson, J. McKeen Cattell and H. W. L. Dana.

Boas, with his customary forthrightness, refused to be silenced. When Columbia University invited its students to report to it on opinions expressed in their classes by faculty members he prepared a statement of his views, read this to his classes on March 7, 1917, and offered to provide a copy to anyone who wished to forward it to the Trustees. Scanned from the perspective of three decades, one wonders how this statement, "Preserving Our Ideals," and republished in part under the title "Patriotism" in the volume of his non-scientific contributions, could ever have been regarded as other than a tightly-argued, intellectual presentation of idealistic principles. Yet at the time it was a courageous expression of a dangerous position. Among Boas' reprints are the proofs of an article, the text of this statement to his students, which had been set in type and was ready for the presses of the New York *Evening Post*. Its editor, Oswald Garrison Villard, was scarcely a man to be accused of lack of courage in the face of popular opposition. Yet the tensions of the moment were too great, and he could not risk publishing the statement Boas was willing to place on public record. Despite all this, Boas' professorship was never jeopardized, though he did not come through the war and immediate post-war unscathed. His steadfastness and scientific integrity, however, soon afterwards regained for him whatever losses he suffered.

The years between the two World Wars was marked by the rise of racism as a political factor that made it logical for Boas to continue his activities in the field of public debate. This was the time, in the United States, when the books of Madison Grant and Lothrop Stoddard afforded the pseudo-scientific basis for the restriction of immigration of East and South Europeans and Orientals in favor of "Nordic" populations; of the employment of the so-called tests of general intelligence, in a manner later repudiated by psychologists, to establish presumed differences in racial abilities; of the recrudescence of the Ku Klux Klan and the aggressive propagation of eugenist doctrines. Against all these Boas spoke out with the authentic voice of the scientist, yet with the passion that the misuse of science always aroused in him. No better instance of this could be had than in his letter to the New York *Times* in 1924, entitled "Lo, the Poor Nordic!" in which he protested against the claims advanced by Henry Fairfield Osborn, the palaeontologist, head of the American Museum of Natural History, regarding the innate superiority of the "Nordic" race.

In the United States, the forces combatting racism were reinforced by the basic equalitarian tradition of American thought. In Germany, however, the rise of Hitler brought the full power of governmental sanction into play on the side of the racists. Boas' voice was raised in the country of his birth as it was in the country of his adoption. In the *Frankfurter Zeitung* of 1926 there appeared his article, "Die Frage der Rassenreinheit," republished in the German journal *Urania* the same year. His address on the occasion of the award to him in 1931 of an honorary Doctorate of Medicine by the University of Kiel, on the fiftieth anniversary of his having been granted his original degree, was entitled "Rasse und Kultur."

On March 27, 1933, he published his open letter to von Hindenburg protesting against his acceptance of Hitler; later that year appeared the article which, of everything he wrote, achieved perhaps the widest circulation, "Aryans and non-Aryans." The German version, distributed by the anti-Nazi underground, is printed on tissue-thin paper, the better to be concealed as it was passed surreptitiously from hand to hand. It appeared in various English versions, and Spanish translations were brought out in cities as far removed as Buenos Aires and Havana. At the age of eighty he travelled to Paris to present a paper at the International

Population Congress; he publicly resigned his honorary membership in the Munich Academy; and publicly answered a communication from a German anthropologist that ended "Heil Hitler" in a way that caused it to be reprinted inside a travel circular for clandestine distribution inside Germany.

If Boas, during the First World War, had shown a devotion to the land of his birth, these activities make it patent that this devotion was no means a blind one. After that war, and before the rise of Hitler, he gave long hours to raising funds to reestablish German art, letters and science. Through his efforts, and almost single-handed, files of American scholarly and scientific periodicals broken during the war, to which German libraries could not afford to subscribe because of the inflation, were brought up to date and continued. When Walter Damrosch, in despair, gave up the task of raising funds to save the Berlin Philharmonic Orchestra, Boas succeeded in collecting the necessary amount. But all this was put aside when authoritarianism, based on a false philosophy of race, struck. For in the case of Boas it struck doubly; it challenged all he stood for as a scientist and citizen, and it came the closer home because, as one of Jewish origin, his many relatives in Germany were among the proscribed.

In his latter years, he became concerned with certain dangers in American life he felt were reflexes of the growing tensions in the European scene. He intensified his support of academic freedom, of civil liberties, and other unpopular causes. Though he was a political independent as far as party affiliation went, in his political sympathies he leaned toward a variety of socialism common among Nineteenth Century liberals. He was obviously no Marxist—we have seen how vigorously he rejected any simplistic explanation of social phenomena, whose complexity none realized better than he. Any determinism, economic no less than geographical or racial, was uncongenial to his thinking. "I do not wish to deny that the economic conflict may be a contributing cause that accentuates the pre-existing feeling of the contrast between whites and Negroes," he wrote in 1921. "It would, however, be an error to seek in these sources the fundamental cause for the antagonism; for the economic conflict, as well as other conflicts, presupposes the social recognition of the classes."

Rather, he was the intellectual, devoted to the free play of thought as manifested in research, teaching and writing, and in terms of democratic equality of access to learning and of the expression of ideas. "It has always seemed to me," he wrote in 1939, in *The American Teacher*, "that if I agree with a person in regard to one specific problem in which we wish to cooperate, his political, religious or social views in regard to other matters are irrelevant. . . . By concentrating our attention upon the main issues of our program and stoutly declining to have other issues brought in we shall grow in unity and in power." Yet the power thus achieved, he insisted, must be held by general consent. "We shall always insist on the right to educate our youth to a clear understanding of the problems of our times, and in order to be able to do so we demand the fullest freedom for the teacher. We shall be prepared to defend it against all attacks, no matter from what side they come. If a radical party should try to restrain us in the same way as do those who do not understand that society is always changing, they would find us as unalterably opposed as we are now to the forces that fear in every free word a danger to the public weal."

5

Boas became emeritus professor in 1937, but his retirement ended neither his scientific productivity nor his struggle against the forces of totalitarianism and the proponents of racism. The unremitting energy he had given to his work exacted its inevitable price from his tiring body; a long-term cardiac condition increasingly placed restrictions on his activity. Yet the psychological set of many years was not to be denied, and his accomplishments during the remaining five years of his life might well have been those of a far younger man.

This period saw the publication of the revision of *The Mind of Primitive Man*, of his volume of collected scientific papers, of the textbook he edited, of the third volume of the *Handbook of American Indian Languages*, of a volume of Kwakiutl tales. His contributions to scholarly journals continued—an answer to continuing criticisms of his study of immigrants, further papers on growth and development, reviews of current books. He worked steadily over the Northwest Coast linguistic data which earlier demands on his time had not permitted him to analyze, and began to prepare the volume on Kwakiutl ethnography that was to bring together his observations of many years on the life of this people. These years, too, find him assuming the melancholy task of writing the obituary notices of two of those whose long association with him in research had cemented some of his closest bonds of personal friendship, Waldemar Bogoras and Elsie Clews Parsons—the last of such duties he was to perform for his associates, and for the all too many students he outlived.

Writing was only a part of these later activities. Monthly, he brought together the linguists of the New York area for discussion of problems of mutual interest. He delivered the principal speech at the celebration of the centenary of the American Ethnological Society. When fatal illness prevented Edward Sapir, one of the greatest among his students, from delivering his presidential address before the American Anthropological Association, Boas spoke in his place. And, continuously, he lectured to non-scientific groups on the nature and meaning of race and the dangers of authoritarianism, driving himself beyond the limits of his now frail strength to bring his vast knowledge and prestige to the support of the values by which he had ordered his own life; and which, disregarded, he was convinced would destroy the means for attaining that full existence toward which his research had shown him man had been groping for millennia.

His death came suddenly, on December 21, 1942. It occurred during a luncheon he gave at the Columbia Faculty Club for Paul Rivet, head of the Musée de l'Homme of Paris, another friend and anthropological colleague of many years, who had been driven into exile by the German occupation and Vichy compliance with its demands. Rivet has written a moving account of what occurred in the periodical *Renaissance,* published in New York during the war years by French and Belgian scholars who took refuge there. The talk at the luncheon had been of earlier days, of anthropology, of the war. It had moved to the question of how to combat the false philosophy of racism, when Boas, with a comment on the need to press its exposure whenever and wherever possible, and without a further sound, fell over backwards in his chair, dead.

Because it was during wartime, and scientific and other meetings were curtailed by restrictions on travel, the societies he had helped form and nourish to maturity could not hold special sessions in his honor. As an obituary for him, the American Anthropological Association published a Memoir in place of the customary article in its journal. And such was his achievement that six of his associates and ex-students were needed to tell the tale of his work in the various divisions of the discipline, while the list of the titles he published, his personal bibliography, required more than forty pages.

Because of his eclecticism, his contribution to the development of anthropology and through it to shaping the currents of general thought are not simple to enumerate. To his science he gave, in addition to massive accumulations of facts, basic methodological and theoretical insights, while his many critical analyses freed those who succeeded him from the need to explore paths which lead to propositions that would confuse, rather than clarify, the aims of the discipline. To the thinking of his time he gave a firm scientific support for tolerance toward racial and cultural differences, in terms so well reasoned and documented that much of what he stood for has moved into common thought, its source unsuspected by most of those who follow it.

That his contribution was so substantial, and his influence so great, must be attributed in largest measure to his willingness to admit the validity of any problem of human life and thought as a subject for study, yet never to commit himself to an answer unless scientific proof was forthcoming. As a scientist, his principles were impeccable, his approach rigorous, his research designs elegant. His scientific testament cannot be better phrased than in the concluding paragraph of his final contribution, presented only a few months before his death and published posthumously: "Reviewing the development of anthropology as a whole I think we may rejoice in the many new lines of research that have been taken up. That many of the new methods need improvement is obvious but unavoidable in new, untested lines of approach. There is perhaps some danger that, engrossed in the difficult psychological problems involved in the analysis of culture, we may forget the importance of the general historical problem with which our science started, but I am certain that with the broadening of our view the varied approaches to an understanding of the history of mankind will be harmoniously elaborated and lead us to a better understanding of our own society."

BIBLIOGRAPHIC NOTE

The following list includes only Boas' larger works. His full bibliography, of some 625 titles, is to be found in the memorial to him published by the American Anthropological Association, as No. 61 of its Memoir series, part 2 of the July-September issue of the *American Anthropologist* (vol. 45, no. 3). Except for various obituary notices in professional journals, this Memoir, entitled *Franz Boas, 1858–1942*, with chapters dealing with the man and the several aspects of his work by A. L. Kroeber, Ruth Benedict, Murray B. Emeneau, Melville J. Herskovits, Gladys A. Reichard and J. Alden Mason, is the only biographical source extant. Boas' unpublished manuscripts, especially in the field of American Indian linguistics, were acquired by the American Philosophical Society, Philadelphia. His scientific library and vast collection of reprints, including the complete file of his own articles which he kept, are in Deering Library, Northwestern University.

Beiträge zur Erkenntniss der Farbe des Wassers (Inaugural-Dissertation zu Erlangung der philosophischen Doctorwürde). Kiel, 1881.

The Central Eskimo (Sixth Annual Report of the Bureau of American Ethnology, 1884–85). Washington, 1888.

Indianische Sagen von der Nord-Pacifischen Küste Amerikas. Berlin, 1895.

The Social Organization and the Secret Societies of the Kwakiutl Indians (Report of the U. S. National Museum for 1895, pp. 311–738). Washington, 1897.

(With Clark Wissler). *Statistics of Growth* (Report of the U. S. Commissioner of Education for 1904, pp. 25–132). Washington, 1905.

Anthropology (Columbia University Lectures on Science, Philosophy and Art, 1907–1908, no. 10). New York, 1908.

The Kwakiutl of Vancouver Island (Publications of the Jesup North Pacific Expedition, vol. 5, part 2: pp. 301–522). New York, 1909.

Handbook of American Indian Languages, Part 1, with illustrative sketches by Roland B. Dixon, P. E. Goddard, William Jones and Truman Michelson, John R. Swanton, and William Thalbitzer. (Bureau of American Ethnology, Bulletin 40, part 1; *contributed:* Preface: pp. v-vi; Introduction: pp. 1–83; Tsimshian: pp. 283–422; Kwakiutl: pp. 423–558; Chinook: pp. 559–678). Washington, 1911. Part 2, Washington, 1922. Part 3, New York, 1938. Part 4, New York, 1941.

Changes in Bodily Form of Descendants of Immigrants. Senate Document 208, 1911, 61st Congress, 2d Session. Washington, 1911. Reprinted New York, 1912.

The Mind of Primitive Man. New York, 1911. Revised Edition, New York, 1938.

Kultur und Rasse. Leipzig, 1914. Second Edition, 1922.

Kutenai Tales: together with texts collected by Alexander Francis Chamberlain (Bureau of American Ethnology, Bulletin 59). Washington, 1918.

Ethnology of the Kwakiutl (Bureau of American Ethnology, 35th Annual Report, parts 1 and 2). Washington, 1921.

Contributions to the Ethnology of the Kwakiutl (Columbia University Contributions to Anthropology, no. 3). New York, 1925.

Keresan Texts (Publications of the American Ethnological Society, vol. 8, Parts 1 and 2). New York, 1925 and 1928.

Primitive Art (Instituttet for Sammenlignende Kulturforskning, Series B, vol. 8). Oslo and Cambridge (Mass.), 1927.

Materials for the Study of Inheritance in Man (Columbia University Contributions to Anthropology, no. 6). New York, 1928.

Anthropology and Modern Life. New York, 1928. London, 1929. Revised edition, New York, 1932.

Religion of the Kwakiutl (Columbia University Contributions to Anthropology, no. 10, Parts 1 and 2). New York, 1930.

Kwakiutl Culture as Reflected in Mythology (Memoirs of the American Folk-Lore Society, no. 28). New York, 1935.

General Anthropology (Contributed: Introduction: pp. 1–6; Biological Premises: pp. 16–23; Race: pp. 95–123; Language: pp. 124–145; Invention: pp. 238–281; Literature, Music and Dance: pp. 589–608; Music and Folk-Lore: pp. 609–626; Methods of Research: pp. 666–686). New York, 1938.

Race Language and Culture (Collected writings). New York, 1938.

Kwakiutl Tales (Columbia University Contributions to Anthropology, no. 26, part 2). New York, 1943.

Race and Democratic Society (Collected addresses and papers for lay audiences). New York, 1945.

CHRONOLOGY

1858   —Born at Minden, Westphalia, Germany (July 9).
1877–81—Study at Universities of Heidelberg, Bonn and Kiel.
1881   —Receives degree of Doctor of Philosophy (major in physics, minor in geography), Faculty of Philosophy, Kiel.
1881–82—Service in German army.
1883–84—Expedition to the Eskimo of Baffinland.
1884–85—First trip to United States.
1885   —Appointed Assistant, Royal Ethnographic Museum, Berlin; Docent (in geography), University of Berlin; field work among Bella Coola.
1887   —Appointed to staff of *Science*; married Marie A. E. Krackowizer.
1888   —Begins work on Indians of North Pacific Coast under auspices of Committee of British Association for the Advancement of Science; appointed Docent (in anthropology), Clark University.
1892   —Appointed Chief Assistant (anthropology), World Columbian Exposition.
1894   —Appointed Curator (anthropology), Field Museum, Chicago.
1896   —Appointed Assistant Curator (ethnology and somatology), American Museum of Natural History, New York; appointed Lecturer (physical anthropology), Columbia University.
1899   —Appointed Professor of Anthropology, Columbia University.

1901 —Appointed Curator of Anthropology, American Museum of Natural History; Honorary Philologist, Bureau of American Ethnology, Washington.

1905 —Resigns from American Museum of Natural History.

1908–25—Editor, *Journal of American Folk-Lore.*

1910–12—In Mexico, with International School of American Archaeology and Ethnology.

1911 —Study of head-form for the Immigration Commission, U. S. Senate, completed.

1914 —Operation for cancerous growth on cheek; field work in Porto Rico.

1917 —Founded *International Journal of American Linguistics.*

1925 —Lectures on primitive art at Institute for the Comparative Study of Culture, Oslo.

1927 —Lectures at New School for Social Research, New York, on anthropology and modern life.

1928 —President, XXIII International Congress of Americanists.

1931 —President, American Association for the Advancement of Science.

1937 —Retires from professorship at Columbia; attends Congrès International de la Population, Paris.

1942 —Dies at luncheon given for Professor Paul Rivet, December 21.

SELECTIVE INDEX